The Fine Line between a GROOVE and a RUT

HOW TO AVOID A SALES SLUMP AND RE-ENERGIZE YOUR MARKETING TEAM!

G.D. KITTREDGE, III

WME BOOKS
a division of
Windsor Media Enterprises, LLC
Rochester, New York
USA

There's a Fine Line between a **GROOVE** and a **RUT**

Copyright © 2005 by G.D. Kittredge III
All rights reserved.

ISBN 0-9765304-4-9

Cover Design: Karin Marlett Choi
Page Layout/Design: Tom Collins

Published by:
    WME Books
    Windsor Media Enterprises, LLC
    Rochester, New York
    USA

Available online at: **www.WMEBooks.com**
as well as other booksellers and distributors worldwide

Special Sales:

This and other WME Books titles are available at special discounts for bulk purchases, for use in sales promotions, or as premiums. Special editions, including personalized covers, excerpts of existing books, and corporate imprints, can be created in large quantities for special needs or projects.

For more information, please contact:
Special Book Orders
Windsor Media Enterprises, LLC
150 Lucius Gordon Drive
West Henrietta, NY 14586

info@wmebooks.com

To Sally, Tad, and Christopher

For giving me my most cherished possessions,
their love and support.

And to Barry, Bill, Cheryl, Fran, Jim,
Patricia, Paul, Scott, Suzanne

and all the other members of the USG.

Table of Contents

- ... Foreword — 1
- ... Introduction — 5
- 1 - Selling 101 — 11
- 2 - I'm Fine. How Are You? — 19
- 3 - A Picture Says a Thousand Words — 25
- 4 - A Fabulous Way to Tell Your Story — 33
- 5 - Cold Calling is for Dummies — 43
- 6 - It Starts with Getting the Appointment — 55
- 7 - The Selling Agenda — 69
- 8 - Establishing Credibility — 79
- 9 - The Sales Presentation — 85
- 10 - The Power of Testimonials — 91
- 11 - Creating a Reason to Come Back — 97
- 12 - How to Ask the Big Question — 101
- 13 - Twenty-One Fine Line Indicators — 113
- 14 - The Rules of the Game — 123
- 15 - Three Things — 131
- ... About the Author — 137

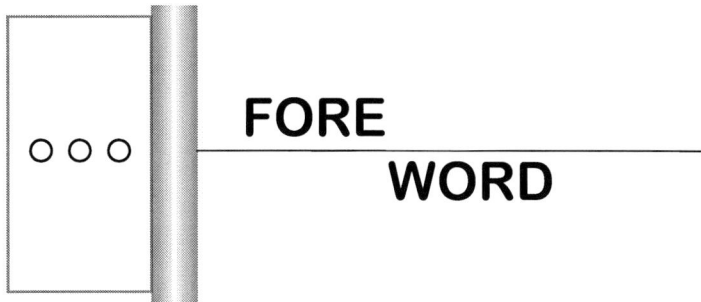

FOREWORD

How does one come to write a book, especially when they have never written one before? It has been said, although I do not know who said it, that there is a book in each of us.

For years I have suggested to many of my colleagues and friends that they ought to write a book. I have a number of friends with extraordinary, creative minds. They are perfect candidates for writing entertaining fiction. Others who have particular expertise, interest and experience, albeit in business, the arts, travel, whatever, seemed to me to be authors in waiting. So I encouraged all of them to pursue something that they had never done before.

Curiously, I had never encouraged myself to do the same thing. That was, until a little over a year ago.

I was doing some volunteer work for a business-oriented, not-for-profit organization when one of the organization leaders asked if I would be a presenter at an upcoming seminar/workshop they were planning. The workshop was to be attended by approximately 30 business owners who wanted to learn how they could

There's a Fine Line between a GROOVE and a RUT

promote their businesses and attract clients, with only a limited marketing budget.

I agreed to submit an outline of what I would talk about and, if they liked it and it fit with the workshop theme, then I would do the workshop. The outline was approved, putting me on the schedule for the next workshop.

As the workshop date approached, I began to think more seriously about what I was going to say. It had to be entertaining, interactive and provide each of the audience members with some lasting value.

Well, that workshop agenda unexpectedly turned into this book. As the content began to unfold, I found it beginning to take on a life of its own.

Then, as I moved from one chapter to the next, my goal became just to finish the book. I've met a number of people who have started books then put them on a back burner where they still remain. Finishing my project became the primary challenge I was determined to meet.

Once finished, my next goal was to get my book published.

After all, having put in the effort to collect and organize the fruits of my years of experience, I thought I should give other people a chance to read the results. I discovered that with today's technology, publishing has become much more author-friendly. It makes no difference whether your book is the next best-selling novel or winds up as a gift to your family and friends, anyone who has the desire to write can become a member in good standing in the universal author's club, using today's print-on-demand technology.

Now that I have accomplished my book-writing and publishing goal, will I write another? I don't know. But I do know that I will encourage anyone who has even the faintest desire to write a book to do so. And I hope they find it as personally rewarding as I have.

G. D. Kittredge III

There's a Fine Line between a GROOVE and a RUT

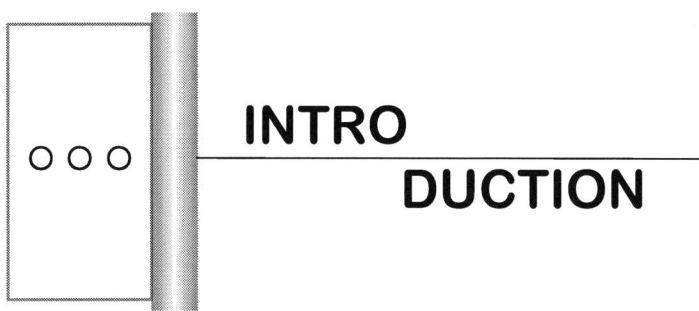

INTRODUCTION

There ***is*** a fine line between being in a groove and being in a rut. Quite possibly you have experienced crossing over this fine line at one time or another. I know I have.

What works so successfully one day, or for many weeks or months in a row, suddenly doesn't appear to work at all. At one point you can't do anything wrong - everything seems to fall into place. Then, for no apparent reason, the results abruptly change. Success disappears.

The goals that you once thought achievable have now become a challenge. You're in a struggle. Simply put, you're in a rut.

How did you get there? And more importantly, how can you get out of it?

Professional athletes experience crossing the fine line many times throughout their careers. Golfers, playing at

There's a Fine Line between a GROOVE and a RUT

the top of their game, winning tournaments and gaining consistent top ten finishes, suddenly seem to lose the touch. Birdies turn into bogies. Makeable putts fail to drop. They begin missing the weekend cuts. Baseball players, on torrid hitting streaks for several weeks, suddenly go into batting slumps.

It happens to all of us - including your sales force.

Your top sales performers for years suddenly fall into mediocrity. Your star player last year now struggles to make quota. Have these stars lost their abilities? Highly unlikely. Have they crossed over that fine line between a groove and a rut? Most probably. Is there something you, as their employer or sales manager, can do about it? Yes, there is.

And that's why I have written this book.

Anticipating when one of your sales people is approaching that fine line, slipping from that groove they were in toward a potential rut, is one of the most important assessments you, as their manager, can make. Successfully pro-acting to avoid this fall and shift performance back toward its peak level is unquestionably the most important managerial function you can perform.

Unfortunately in many instances, the person who slips below the fine line is the last person to realize that he or she is in a rut. Often it is much easier for an outside observer, not only to identify when someone else is in a rut, but to detect earlier when someone is beginning to slide toward that fine line heading toward a rut.

Introduction

There are a number of reasons why any of your sales representatives may fall into a rut. Although some of these reasons may be out of your control, others you do have some control over. As their sales manager you must learn to recognize the reasons you can influence and take steps to minimize their impact.

Observing people in other walks of life who perform at the top of their professions can be a valuable exercise.

These people always seem to stay above that fine line, almost always seem to be in a groove. And, when they occasionally fall below the line, they have that wonderful ability to find and correct their shortcomings and rise back to the top.

If you observe these people more closely, it's not difficult to learn their secret. It's not difficult to understand how they maintain a high performance level and sustain their positive momentum.

Tiger Woods and Annika Sorenstam are considered two of the best golfers in the world. Like most of us, they have their good days and bad. But why is it that their good days greatly outweigh the bad? Why is it that when they cross the fine line from a groove and fall into a rut, it's only temporary? Why does it not take them very long to bounce back? Why, when they have a rare couple of bad rounds that knocks them out of contention, within a week or two they are back on top playing at the very highest level?

It's because that even though they are among the best at their trade, they never stop learning how to improve themselves in their profession. It's not uncommon to see

There's a Fine Line between a GROOVE and a RUT

either one of them, after playing what most of us would call a very good golf round, immediately head to the putting green or the driving range to practice.

They and other top golfers do not hesitate to talk with other golf professionals about their performances. They continue to ask for criticism, insights, and tips from other pros and trainers on where they can make improvements. They are constantly trying new equipment, seeking better tools for their trade. Most importantly, they do not hesitate to try new ideas if they believe it might help.

In short, consistent top performers are **constantly learning new ways to improve** their performances, even though they are already considered by many to be the best in the world at what they do!

Many people believe that selling, just as in sports, has a built-in scorecard. And I agree. It is relatively easy to evaluate sales performance by comparing one's sales successes from one period of time to another, or by comparing an individual's success with his or her peers.

Are their sales increasing? Are they on or above target? Is their new account production meeting goals? Are new product sales up? These and other factors are typical indicators of how well your sales people are performing.

However, in some instances historical numbers do not tell the complete story of whether or not your sales representative is beginning to lose that edge.

When the numbers begin to indicate a decline, you may already be months late in reacting to correct the problem.

I have designed this book to be a guide to help you inject some solid selling and communication skills into your periodic sales training sessions. Each interactive session I discuss will enable your meetings to become more meaningful, constructive and educational, all aimed at improving your sales representatives' sales performance.

Throughout my selling and management career, I have used, and still use, all of these communication and selling skills. They have helped me stay above the fine line. They will work for you and your selling team.

In fact, I encourage you to share all of these ideas with every employee you have. As part of your business team, each of your employees has an unlimited number of opportunities to promote your business. Now, you can show them how to do it.

I believe that you will be surprised at how easy these skills are to understand and use. So easy in fact, you'll wonder why everyone who is in sales or is trying to promote his or her business isn't using them. But the truth is, they aren't.

Find out for yourself. After you read this book, observe how many people actually use just some of the communication and presentation skills I talk about.

How many of your sales people do?

There's a Fine Line between a GROOVE and a RUT

If you help your sales people better communicate your message, they will have an enormous impact upon your business success.

As you prepare to read this book, ask yourself these questions:

- Is every sales rep in your company constantly learning new ways to improve their game?
- More importantly, are you as their manager consistently critiquing and offering guidance, insights, and tips to keep them in the groove?
- Have you been looking for creative and interactive ways to stimulate your sales meetings and ways to incorporate some solid technique skills into your training sessions?

If you strive to provide every opportunity you can for your sales organization and employees, if you want them to perform at their peak levels, if you want to help those who appear to be struggling and guide them back in a positive direction, you will find *There's A Fine Line Between A Groove And A Rut* a great place to start.

1 SELLING 101

I'd like to begin by telling you a story about a recent college graduate. This young woman, looking to start her first job in the "real world," has applied for a sales position with a local company.

The company has invited her in for an initial interview and she has arrived at the appointed time to speak with Mr. Barker, the sales manager.

The interview begins:

Mr. Barker: "Ms. Wilson, thank you for coming in today to talk about our sales position. To help me learn more about your background, would you tell me a little about what you did in college?"

Ms. Wilson: "Thank you for meeting with me, Mr. Barker. I would be pleased to share with you what I learned and did during my four years there. Last Spring I graduated with a Bachelor of Science Degree in Professional Selling. It was an exciting and enlightening learning experience. The curriculum provided a great framework and understanding regarding the principles and techniques that are used to be successful in sales."

Mr. Barker: "Please go on."

Ms. Wilson: "Our professors, many of whom are working business professionals, taught us how to research and learn about the company we might become employed with. We learned how to gain an in-depth understanding of the products and services we would be selling and what makes that company and its products stand out from the competition. We learned how to accurately and succinctly articulate our employer's marketing message to prospective clients, how to gain appointments, what to do on an initial sales call and how to follow up on future calls."

Mr. Barker: "That's very interesting."

Ms. Wilson: "I particularly liked the courses that taught us how to avoid customer indecision and how to obtain referrals and testimonials. Most importantly, we learned the best ways to use those referrals and testimonials to better retain current customers and to attract new clients. In addition, we studied time management, sales call planning and effective note-taking. Our role-playing exercises were very helpful in increasing our listening and speaking skills."

Chapter 1
Selling 101

Mr. Barker: "Were you able to gain any actual selling experience?"

Ms. Wilson: "Yes. During the first semester of my senior year, our class created our own product with the objective of selling it to the business community. Our goal was to develop a job creation collaborative with area businesses and our college. Each business was asked to contribute $2000 to the program to help funding, provide 20 hours of volunteer business expertise from one or more of their executives and to offer one internship to a college student."

Mr. Barker: "What role did you play?"

Ms. Wilson: "I was a sales representative. I analyzed the market, targeted specific companies, developed my own sales strategy, scheduled appointments with the decision-makers and made sales presentations."

Mr. Barker: "Were you successful in your sales efforts?"

Ms. Wilson: "Over a two-month period, I obtained commitments from seven area companies."

Mr. Barker: "Congratulations."

Ms. Wilson: "Oh, and one company offered me an intern sales position with them during my second semester. I was able to work with a number of their top sales people, making calls with them and learning first hand how to be the best at selling. While researching your company, Mr. Barker, I became very excited about the new product line you have been field-testing. I've identified three market niches you currently do not sell to that, I think, would be a great source for new customers."

Mr. Barker: "What college did you say you graduated from?"

Boy, would I have loved to have had an applicant like that young woman apply for one of my sales positions. I think I would have even created a position for her.

Unfortunately, such a person has never knocked on my door. I doubt if you have ever interviewed such a candidate either.

Have you ever met someone who had a college degree in professional selling? I know I haven't.

In fact, I would be hard pressed to identify any college or university that offers any in-depth curricula in professional selling. There are many marketing and public speaking courses, and there are a variety of business management courses. But, there are not many (if any) courses that teach how to effectively sell something to somebody.

From all the people I have hired to work for me as a sales representative and the hundreds I have interviewed, I have never met anyone who studied professional selling in college. Lots of marketing people, many liberal arts, some engineers, economics majors — the list goes on — but no selling.

And that's not the way it should be.

Whether you're trying to sell a product to a new client, attempting to enlist volunteers to join your committee, or trying to convince your spouse that it's time to get a new mattress for your bed, you need to know how to sell your ideas.

Everyone can benefit from learning basic selling skills and being able to communicate in a clear, courteous, and persuasive manner.

I have attended a number of sales training seminars over the years. Several of them have been conducted by prestigious and nationally recognized sales training companies. Many of the sessions were multiple days.

Although much of the information I learned was helpful, in most instances I came away as much confused as anything else.

These courses presented fairly detailed selling procedures and offered in-depth analysis. I could learn 24 different ways to close a sale. I could learn 15 or more ways to overcome objections. If I had had an exceptional memory, I might have been able to remember all the techniques laid out before me.

However, what I found was that in the real selling world the scenarios never played out the same way they did in the classroom. I came away from most of those elaborate training programs thinking that if I forgot step five in my 12-step presentation, I was dead.

There's a **Fine Line** between a **GROOVE** and a **RUT**

If you are currently managing a sales force, ask yourself these questions:

- Where and how did each of your sales people learn how to sell?
- Did they take special training courses?
- Did they have a mentor somewhere in their sales career?
- Or did they just create their own style of selling all by themselves from the school of trial and error?

If you're a small business owner and do not have a sales force, then you probably are the person who creates sales for your company. Where did *you* learn how to sell?

Interesting questions?

If you have recently hired a new sales representative, chances are that he or she does not have a degree in selling. Chances are that none of your sales people have college degrees in professional selling either.

And if they don't take it upon themselves to learn new skills, or if you are not teaching them new skills, they most likely have not learned anything new about selling since you hired them.

Wouldn't it be nice if you could enroll each of them in an on-going training course?

Fine Line
RULE # 1

The best person to teach new ways to improve your employees' performance is **you**.

Over the remaining chapters in this book, you will see how easy it is to introduce your own ongoing sales techniques training program.

As they learn from you, they will be able to use their new skills with the very next client or prospect they meet.

It's a program that will be personally rewarding to each of your sales representatives and to you as well. You will immediately be able to see the results of your efforts. Welcome to your own personalized Selling 101 course.

Let's get started.

There's a Fine Line between a GROOVE and a RUT

2 I'M FINE. HOW ARE YOU?

How many times, when you meet someone, do they ask how you are? It's a typical greeting we all use when we greet someone.

And the usual response is, "I'm fine. How are you?"

How many times, when you see someone, are you asked what you do or, more importantly, what the company you own or work for does?

Probably not as often as you would like, if you are trying to promote your business. That's particularly true if it is a new business, or if you are trying to increase the number of customers you have.

But you can change that.

There is something that you can do right now and something that you can easily teach your sales people that will result in both them and you being asked to talk about your business every time you meet someone.

There is a sure-fire way to get people to ask what you do, what your company does, what new products or services you've just introduced, or what that new business you've just started is all about. They will ask you almost anything you want them to ask you.

Think about the following idea which, if you begin using it and train your sales people to use it, will become a great way to promote your business in a cordial and receptive manner. It's an idea that will create awareness among your contacts, friends, associates and potential new clients.

Very often when we run into someone on the street that we know, or see a neighbor over the backyard fence, or see a colleague at a meeting or social event, we greet him or her with, "Hi Bob" or "Hi Susan. How are you?"

Again, the likely answer: "I'm fine. How are you?"

If we respond with usual, "I'm fine," the conversation will either move on to something else, or simply end as you part company.

Be aware. Opportunity just knocked on your door — and you missed it!

Fine Line
RULE # 2

Seize every opportunity to promote your business and what you do.

Chapter 2
I'm Fine. How Are You?

I'd like to suggest a different response to the many "how-are-yous" we hear every day.

Greeting someone is an ideal time for

- anyone who has recently started a business,
- for someone who has recently joined a business,
- for someone who has just received a promotion or taken on a new assignment,
- for someone whose business has just introduced a new product,
- for anyone who has something newsworthy to say about their work or their business,

to start a meaningful and potentially rewarding conversation.

When someone asks you how you are, it's the perfect time to talk about your business.

Try this response and see what happens.

Let's say that you have recently started your own business and you meet Bob, a business acquaintance whom you haven't seen for a few months. You greet him with, "Hi Bob. How are you?"

Bob replies "I'm fine. How are you?"

Instead of saying "Fine," you respond with "Bob, I just started my own business and I feel great!"

Let me repeat that:

"Bob, I just started my own business and I feel great!"

What happens next?

Bob will most likely reply with something like "Really. What kind of company did you start?" or "What type of business are you in?"

You have just seized the opportunity to talk about you and your business.

Here's another example:

"Hi, Bob. How are you?"

"I'm fine, George, how are you?"

"Bob, my company has just introduced a new product, and I am really excited about how it will help our customers."

"Really, George? What kind of product is it?"

I have used this type of greeting hundreds of times when I wanted to start a specific conversation. It works almost every time.

Instead of those meaningless "how-are-you — fine" discussions, I've had some very meaningful conversations about what I am doing, or what my business is doing. Often the conversation concludes with an unsolicited offer from my companion to help spread the word.

Having just written and published this book, I would love everyone to buy it. So I seize every opportunity I can to tell people about it.

When someone greets me these days and asks me how I am, I often reply with, "I've just published a book and I'm very excited about it."

Chapter 2
I'm Fine. How Are You?

Their response invariably is something like, "That's great! What's the book about?"

I'm off and running.

I see perhaps twenty or more people a day that I'm not expecting to see. That gives me 20 opportunities to talk about this book and my work.

Do your sales people meet 20 or more people a day? Don't let them miss all those opportunities. Each one is a chance to tell another person about your business and what they do.

Try this training exercise with your sales force at an upcoming sales meeting.

At the beginning of the meeting, walk over to three or four representatives in succession and ask each to greet you with, "Hi. How are you?"

You reply with, "I'm fine, how are you?"

See how many of them answer, "Fine," or something similar.

Then teach them how to turn this greeting into a meaningful discussion that promotes the business and work they are in.

Have them practice in teams of two, out loud, with the rest of the group listening and observing until everyone's responses become almost second nature. You will be amazed at how often such conversations will turn into business opportunities for them.

Think of it. Twenty new business opportunities each day. If you have a five-person sales team, that could mean over 500 possible new business-networking opportunities each week. All from a simple greeting.

So, now that you know how to prompt someone you meet into asking you to explain what you and your company do, how do you answer that question?

How do your sales people answer?

You have just been offered a wonderful opportunity to positively promote your business. Unfortunately, very little time is ever spent on practicing and responding with a great answer. Often, such a question as, "What do you do?" can catch you off guard, making your answer vague or incomplete.

Without either of you knowing it, your listener may not understand some of the words you use to describe your business. If your message is not clear, your opportunity is lost.

But there is something you can do to ensure that the next time you — or anyone in your company — is asked what your company does, you'll be ready to use these opportunities to their fullest advantage.

Learning how to respond to "how are you" will even make you **look forward** to the next time the question comes up. I wouldn't be surprised if, after you teach them to respond properly, your sales people begin actively looking for people they can prompt into asking what your company does.

A great tip awaits you in the next chapter.

A PICTURE SAYS A THOUSAND WORDS

Several years ago at a business luncheon I attended, a guest speaker had each of us participate in a simple exercise to introduce ourselves to the group. It was a very effective exercise and left a strong impression on me.

The speaker demonstrated a much better way for each of us to introduce ourselves in a business atmosphere, a way that I have used ever since. I would like you to try this same exercise yourself and share it with your sales force at one of your sales meetings.

I am sure it will have the same affect on you as it did on me.

At the end of the exercise, each of your sales representatives will leave with a totally new way to introduce themselves and your company.

Let's first talk about what, unfortunately, is the normal way people explain what they do. Here is an example.

There's a Fine Line between a GROOVE and a RUT

At a recent association monthly meeting, I spotted a new member and started a conversation with him. I asked him what type of business he was in.

He replied that he was a software consultant.

Unfortunately for him and for me, that told me very little. I'm not even sure if I know exactly what a software consultant does.

Unless he was going to provide me with some more information, I would leave that conversation not really knowing what he did.

So I asked him what type of consulting he did.

His answer was that he was a trouble-shooter for new technology being used in the communications industry. This was a slightly better answer, but it still did not answer my main question.

What did he really do?

You've heard the expression, "Can't see the forest through the trees?"

Sometimes we become so involved in our work and we understand it so well, we unknowingly have difficulty in expressing to others exactly what we do. In an effort to reply with a succinct answer, we give our listener very little valuable information.

Test this theory out with your sales team.

At your next sales meeting, ask each of your sales people to write down what they would say if someone

Chapter 3
A Picture Says a Thousand Words

asked them what their company does. Then have each read their answers to the group.

I have tried this with business owners and managers, and these are some of the answers that I received.

Some people answered with a single sentence.

For example, I recently asked one of the owners of a company that helps build websites (among other services) what his company did.

His answer was, "We provide Internet marketing solutions for small business."

His answer, although accurate (in his mind), told me very little about his company. I was left to figure out what Internet marketing solutions were. I could ask, but if I didn't, his opportunity was lost.

A sales manager told me that his company provided "surface coatings to metal fabrication manufacturers." Once again, not much for me to go on.

Let's use this book as another example. When people find out that I have written a book, the obvious question they ask is, "What's your book about?"

Here's an opportunity for me to create enough interest where the person who has asked the question might like to purchase a copy or perhaps tell someone else who might want to buy 100 copies.

Wouldn't that be great?

> **Fine Line**
> **RULE # 3**
>
> When explaining what you or your company does, create a mental picture for your listener.

Let's say I reply with, "My book is about specific sales techniques that business owners and sales managers can teach their sales force to improve sales performance."

To a degree my answer is correct. But have I really given my listener a good mental picture of what my book is about?

No, I haven't.

My answer has provided somewhat of a blank canvas with lots of empty spaces for my inquirer to fill in.

Chances are his response will be something like, "Oh, that's interesting." And then we move on.

The speaker at that luncheon taught me a better response. She taught me how to begin answering such a question with a question of my own. It goes something like this:

Inquirer: "What is your book about?"

Me: "Have you ever noticed how some professional athletes can at one moment be

Chapter 3
A Picture Says a Thousand Words

winning almost everything and then, for some unknown reason, go into a slump?"

Inquirer: "Oh yeah. I think it happens to most athletes."

Me: "Well, it happens to business people too. Especially sales people. My book is entitled, *There's A Fine Line Between A Groove And A Rut*, and I wrote it for business owners and sales managers. It talks about things managers can do to teach their sales people how to avoid getting into a rut, how to be better communicators, and how to develop better business relationships with their customers. For example, in the second chapter I talk about how you can get people you meet to ask about your business simply by the way you greet them."

Do you see what my answer has done? It has given my inquirer a specific example, a much clearer picture of what my book is about.

Notice that I did not try to tell him or her everything about the book, just a small part of it.

So let's go back to the first example about the company that builds websites and provides other services to small businesses and replay that conversation.

I have a business colleague who owns such a company and here is his reply when I ask him what his company does.

Me: "Henry, what does your company do?"

There's a Fine Line between a GROOVE and a RUT

Henry: "We provide Internet marketing solutions for small and midsize businesses."

Me: "Oh, that's nice."

And that's the end of the conversation. Henry missed a great opportunity to talk about his business. He probably didn't even realize that I still didn't know what he did.

So I showed Henry another way to respond that had a better chance of creating some interest in his business — a better way to create that mental picture.

Me: "Henry, what does your company do?"

Henry: "George, can you imagine how difficult it can sometimes be for a small business with limited resources to build and maintain a viable website that can strongly compete with the bigger companies that are their competitors?"

Me: "Yes, I can."

Henry: "Well, one of the things my company does is offer small business owners an exciting website-building technology that utilizes a large variety of interchangeable templates. All the owner needs to do is supply the content he or she wants to have on their website and, with a little more than a push of a button, select the website format they want to use. Almost immediately, they are able to have a professional website up and running. It costs a lot less money than if they hired a consulting company to come in and build a website from scratch."

Chapter 3
A Picture Says a Thousand Words

Henry has now given me a specific example of something his company does. I have a mental picture. And providing a clear mental picture to a listener is more than likely to create an atmosphere to continue the conversation.

Before we leave this subject, however, I would like to add this additional thought. Listen to how Henry ends his response to me.

> Henry continues: "I'm eager to show business owners how our templates work, how they can be personalized to meet a specific business owners needs and how the owner can benefit. Can you think of anyone you know that I might contact?"

Henry has completed his response with a question of his own. He's asking for some help.

He's asking me to help him connect with a potential client or two that I might know. He's asking for a referral.

We will talk more about asking for referrals later in this book.

Henry's response and ending question is an effective way to keep the conversation focused on what his business does and, at the same time, draw me into the conversation.

Teaching your sales force how to effectively respond when asked what your company does can pay great dividends.

There's a Fine Line between a GROOVE and a RUT

At a future sales meeting ask each of them to write down what your company does. After each sales rep has read his or her response out loud to the group, give them examples of how they could improve their response. You can use the above examples if you wish or create some of your own.

Now ask each participant to pick an aspect of your business they believe offers a good example of your company's capabilities. Have them rewrite and read their responses.

No doubt, you will hear a number of ideas.

Next, have the group critique the new responses and select the ones they feel are the best. Fine tune any they believe need it. And finally, role-play with each participant until they become comfortable expressing their responses verbally.

As a follow-up to the meeting, give each of your sales people written copies of each response developed and selected during the sales meeting and ask them to practice any they wish to use.

Tell each of them that at your next meeting you will ask them to role-play their answers without the use of cue cards.

This is a truly great exercise.

Once they begin using their new responses in real situations, they'll never change back to the old one-line answers. And your business will benefit from it.

4 A FABULOUS WAY TO TELL YOUR STORY

The world today is filled with acronyms. Thanks to technology, as a culture we have become proficient in taking any set of perfectly understandable words and turning them into a series of letters or letters and numbers. A vocabulary that started out with SATs and CPR has become an ever-expanding alphabet soup.

I love listening to high-tech professionals explain their technology to someone. When they finish their explanation, the listener frequently hasn't a clue as to what they were talking about.

Here's an example of a promotional piece I recently read that was written for a high-tech products and services company. "If you are seeking to improve your CRM programs through better SFA integration, perhaps you need to re-consider the ASP model or LAN program you are using. Whether it's CSS, CSR 24/7 or total ERM, our technology can provide you with the software that includes SSL, SSH and SCP to upgrade your IT or MIS operations. The result will be a TMA system you and your MSRs will be proud of."

There's a Fine Line between a GROOVE and a RUT

Kind of takes your breath away, doesn't it?

Acronyms began finding their way into business language during the mid-twentieth century. It started with blue chip companies who, after diversifying their products and services, discovered that their corporate names no longer represented their businesses.

Companies like International Business Machines, National Cash Register, and Minnesota Mining & Manufacturing all changed their names to acronyms. In fact, it was so long ago, I'll bet you can find many people today who do not know what IBM, NCR, or 3M originally stood for.

However, it was the emergence of the technology era that made acronyms into an art form. And the trend has become contagious. Today, businesses invent new acronyms as fast as they create new products.

Here are just a few examples, but the list is almost endless. What use to be called business to business is now B2B. So it seems reasonable to assume that people to people business is now P2P (but, of course, that one's already taken by "peer-to-peer" — think: Napster). Customer service representatives are now called CSRs. Professional sports leagues all use acronyms. MLB, NFL, NBA, PGA and WBA are just a few. Today you work for a CEO, COO, CFO, or perhaps you work in HR. Most web sites today have a Q&A page.

And how many of you play CDs, DVDs, and use a VCR?

If you have the same reaction to acronyms as I do, you will be pleased to know that I present no acronyms in this book.

Chapter 4
A FABulous Way to Tell Your Story

Except one.

When it comes to promoting your business, there is only one acronym you need to remember - **FAB**.

No, it's not the laundry detergent. FAB stands for features, advantages and benefits. And in all my years of marketing, promoting, direct selling and training others to sell, I have not discovered a better way to describe a product, service or business.

Fine Line
RULE # 4

The best way
to tell your story is with
features, advantages,
and benefits.

Ask your sales force how many of them use FABs when talking to a client or prospect. I'm sure that some in the room will not know what you're talking about.

Whether you're selling a million dollar piece of equipment or a $3.00 screwdriver, whether you're promoting a subscription series or your lawn care service program, there is no better way to communicate your message than by presenting the features, advantages and benefits of the products and services you offer.

There's a Fine Line between a GROOVE and a RUT

The use of FABs is an easy method to teach and easy to learn. Once you see the dramatic and positive affect it has on your sales force, you will include a FAB training session on every product and service you offer in your company, as well as everything that your marketing and sales people promote.

So how does it work?

First, let's talk about features.

I would like you to think of a product that you recently purchased for yourself. Perhaps it was a new pair of shoes, some jewelry, or a magazine subscription. The features in the product you purchased are the qualities and attributes that the product possesses.

The product you are thinking about probably has many features. A feature could be the design of the product, how easy it is to maintain, the guarantee that comes with it or any number of factors. No doubt, it was one or more of these product features that attracted you to this product in the first place.

The advantage of a product is how a particular feature of a product works for the customer (to his or her advantage).

For example, the guarantee that came with my magazine subscription stated that if I was not satisfied after receiving three issues, I could cancel my subscription and receive a full refund with no questions asked.

The guarantee was the feature. How the guarantee worked, that I could cancel my subscription and get all of money back, was the advantage.

Chapter 4
A FABulous Way to Tell Your Story

So what is the benefit?

The benefit of a product or service is the result the customer will receive from the feature-advantage. As a result of the magazine subscription guarantee, I could examine the magazine knowing that I could get my money back if I was not satisfied. The benefit to me was that any risk of paying for something I did not want was eliminated.

If I were expressing an FAB to a customer, I might say this:

"Mr. Customer, one of the features of this product is _____. Here is how this feature works to your advantage. And as a result, this is the benefit you will receive."

Or, to state it another way:

"One of the features is..."

"Here is how it works..."

"As a result..."

Here are a couple of examples. Let's assume you manage a fulfillment company that handles the order taking and processing, billing and shipping services for your client companies. Using FABs as a way of promoting your company, you could describe your service in this manner:

"One of the features of our service is our 24-hour tracking system. Here is how that tracking system works. Each order, when received, is electronically coded with a special tracking number that allows us to monitor the exact movement and location of the

There's a Fine Line between a GROOVE and a RUT

merchandise until it reaches its final destination. We are able to automatically locate and track the status of every order 24 hours a day, seven days a week. With our service your orders cannot be lost, can be immediately located while in transit, and will reach your customer on time. As a result, your company will become known for its ability to service its customers."

In this example, the feature is the 24-hour tracking system. The advantage is being able to automatically locate each order no matter where it is in the system, so that customers' orders will not be lost and will be delivered on time. The benefit is a high customer satisfaction rating.

FABs will work on any product or service. Let's use this book again as an example.

"One of the features of this book is the way the author presents the information. Each selling technique discussed in each chapter is presented in a clear and concise manner and includes examples. As a result, the reader will find the information easy to understand and easy to incorporate into their own personal sales training program."

To start your sales people thinking in terms of FABs, set aside a portion of a future sales meeting to develop features, advantages, and benefits for some of the key products and services your company provides and what they sell.

Begin by explaining what FABs are. Features, advantages, benefits.

Chapter 4
A FABulous Way to Tell Your Story

- Features are the qualities or attributes of the product or service.
- Advantages express how each feature works.
- Benefits are the results the customer receives.

Next, as a beginning exercise, choose some examples of products or services your group is familiar with (but not any of the products or services you carry).

Then have the group select one of your examples they would like to create a feature, advantage, benefit profile on. Have them compile a list of features first. Be sure to recognize that a feature offered from the group is really a feature. Often, people will confuse how something works (advantage) with an attribute (feature). Once you have a representative list of features, decide on three features that best represent your product example.

For each of the three features identified, have the group determine an appropriate advantage and a benefit to the customer. Before completing this exercise, get everyone in the room to agree that the three FABs are expressed correctly.

As a final step, have each sales representative select and state, out loud, one of the FABs they have created and continue to go around the room until everyone is comfortable with describing the feature, advantage and benefit of the product.

This is an excellent exercise. You will not find a better way for your sales people to learn how to express, in understandable terms, the most important factors about your products and services.

39

Next, select a couple of products or services that your company offers, and repeat the exercise.

At the end of the sales meeting, pass out FAB sheets on the products/services you have developed during the meeting. These sheets will serve as examples for the homework assignment that you are about to give them.

Prior to ending the session, ask each member of your sales group to select two more products or services they sell. Ask them to prepare a feature/advantage/benefit statement for each product to present to the group. Their presentations will become the framework for an FAB session at your next sales meeting.

At a follow-up sales meeting, the group can critique each FAB example and become comfortable with a whole new way of describing your products and services. I encourage you to role-play as much as possible.

Over time, and after a series of sales meetings, you will have accomplished two wonderful things. First, your sales force will have created effective FAB statements for your most important products and services, something you can use as training tools for future hires.

Second, you will have taught them an effective way to articulate and present your products and services to their customers.

Of course, the real proof is in how effectively your sales people use this new tool to promote and sell. When you travel to your prospects and clients with your sales people, be aware of when and how they use their FABs. Done correctly, it will give your clients the reasons why they should buy from you.

Chapter 4
A FABulous Way to Tell Your Story

Perhaps you do not have a sales force. Perhaps you are a small business just starting out. Perhaps you have just met someone named Frank and told him that you "just started a business and you feel great."

Very likely Frank replied, "That's great. What kind of business are you in?"

After creating a mental picture by asking Frank if he knows about (fill in the type of problem your new business solves), remember Fine Line Rule #4:

"Frank, one of the features of my new business (you fill in the blank). Here's how it works: (you fill in the blank). As a result, my clients will benefit by (you fill in the blank again)."

Oh, and you might close with: "Can you think of one or two people you might suggest I contact?"

There's a Fine Line between a GROOVE and a RUT

5 COLD CALLING IS FOR DUMMIES

There is an extremely popular series of books on the market today written "For Dummies" There's *Cooking For Dummies, Taxes For Dummies* and *Auto Repair For Dummies*. They have even written *Divorce For Dummies*.

In fact, the Internet lists over 1900 titles in the "For Dummies" series. Apparently you can find something on just about any subject imaginable for dummies.

There is, however, one topic I looked for that has not been written about — but should be. Perhaps this chapter could be the start of their next publication. I would call it *Cold Calling For Dummies*.

Because cold calling *is* for dummies.

Whenever I look at employment advertisements in the newspaper-classified sections, I almost always see one or more ads for a sale representative position where they state that "cold calling is required." Take a look at your newspaper. I bet you will find at least one.

There's a Fine Line between a GROOVE and a RUT

Here's a typical cold calling ad:

> Eastside manufacturing company seeks individual to perform inside and outside sales. Must have 3-5 years experience. Cold calling required. Income based on experience. Contact...

When I see these types of ads, I wonder what kind of sales training program they have. Do they hire people, give them some basic product knowledge and then hand them the phone book and say, "Okay, start cold calling?" Now there's a sales strategy.

I guess you have figured out that I am not a big fan of cold calling.

Cold calling is a complete waste of time, energy, and money. What are the odds of picking up the phone, calling someone to sell them your product or service, and hearing them say, "Gee, I'm glad you called. How soon can we get together?"

How many times have you gotten unsolicited phone calls (they are usually at dinner time, right?) and responded positively to their information?

The main point here is that the results of such calls are extremely poor. Some analysts have put the odds at 100 to 1 that cold calling results in a sale.

Think of it. Out of every 100 calls your sales representative makes, maybe one call might generate some business.

Worse than that, some sales people make an even bigger mistake.

Chapter 5
Cold Calling is for Dummies

If your sales people submit sales call reports for personal sales visits they make each week, take a close look at the "results of the call" column. If you read things like "could not see," "not available," "stop in next week," "contact next week," or something similar, you have a problem.

Your sales people are not telephone cold calling. They are committing a bigger sin: cold calling in person.

Not only would I not want to work for a company that required cold calling, I surely would not want my sales representatives wasting all their time (and mine) on such unnecessary and unproductive work.

So, if you don't cold call and prospective clients are not beating your door down, what can you do?

Here's a great suggestion to eliminate cold calling and increase your sales force's ability to generate potential new clients. First, consider these questions.

- What is the most effective way to attract the interest of a prospect?
- If you wanted to contact a prospect by telephone, what would be the most effective way to encourage that person to want to talk to you and listen to what you have to say?

The answer is referrals.

Let me say that again. The answer is referrals.

And how do you get referrals?

The answer is networking. I know this is an overused term, but it works.

There's a Fine Line between a GROOVE and a RUT

If networking is the best way to obtain referrals, where should you have your sales force start? Or, if you have selling responsibilities, where should you start?

A few years ago when I was managing a business unit that comprised over 100 sales reps, I realized that we did not have an acceptable, growing list of "hot prospects" to develop new business.

After assessing the situation, my goal was to have each representative maintain an ongoing list of at least 40 hot prospects at all times. A list where there was an excellent chance of successfully closing a sale within 30-60 days.

Having each representative maintain a list of 40 hot prospects would mean that at any one time the business unit would be working on potentially closing at least 4000 new clients. When one prospect fell off the list, either through successfully closing the sale or not, the goal for the sales representative was to replace that prospect with a new one.

Prior to starting the hot prospect campaign, I estimated the average number of hot prospects in the business unit to be about 15-20 per sales representative. The challenge would be to more than double the size of that list.

Cold calling was not the answer.

I knew that the best way to increase the list of potentially interested prospects was through referrals. Here's what I did.

Chapter 5
Cold Calling is for Dummies

Each representative in the business unit was required to submit periodic sales call reports to their sales managers listing who they called on, what products or services were discussed, the results, etc. Usually these reports were on a weekly basis. New sales representatives might be submitting daily reports as part of their initial training program.

Many of the businesses they contacted were current accounts, which is where I knew we could generate some referrals.

I instructed my sales managers to add one column to the report form that would enable the representative to note one or more referral names they obtained from their customers.

The sales representatives were directed to ask for at least one referral from each of their current accounts prior to ending the sales call. Actually, we asked them to try for two or more referrals.

Acting on the referrals they obtained, each sales rep began to increase the number of hot prospects they were pursuing.

When you think about it, it makes a lot of sense. Who better to provide you with names of others that might like your products or services than those who are already using your products and services?

Let me ask you this: Do you have each of your sales representatives routinely asking for referrals on each of their sales calls?

There's a Fine Line between a GROOVE and a RUT

If so, do you monitor how successful they are at getting referrals? Do you monitor how successfully those referrals result in new clients? If you are not doing all of these things, you should be.

And if all you get out of this book is the realization of what an active referral program can do for your business, then I will consider that I have achieved my objective in writing it.

Obtaining referrals is painless and easy. Here is just how easy it can be:

> Sales representative (finishing a sales call): "Mr. Thompson, before we finish I have a question for you. Your company has been doing business with us for over two years now, is that correct?"
>
> Mr. Thompson: "Yes. I believe that's true."
>
> Sales representative: "Sir, what would you say are the biggest reasons why you use our service?"
>
> Mr. Thompson: "Well, your service has allowed me to divert financial resources to other critical areas, and your work has always been prompt and cost-effective."
>
> Sales representative: "That's great to hear. But let me ask you something. I very much want to meet some new business owners in the area that may not know about us to see if we can help them as we are helping you. Could you suggest a couple of business colleagues that I might contact? Your thoughts would be very helpful to me."

Chapter 5
Cold Calling is for Dummies

Yes, it really is just that easy. The sales representative has very effectively and sincerely asked his or her current customer to help direct them toward additional prospects. The chances are very good that their customer will provide them with one or two names.

I've done it and in most instances, my customers have given me one or two names to contact. Some have even given me more.

I'll never forget during one customer sales visit, his response to my request. He not only gave me a referral, but he picked up the telephone and called that person himself while I was still in his office and arranged an appointment for me. How's that for a positive referral?

Fine Line
RULE # 5

A current customer
will be very receptive to
giving you a referral.
All you need to do is ask.

Numbers tell the story. The business unit that I managed had over 20,000 current accounts. Obtaining on average one referral from each client would mean 20,000 new referrals. Converting just 10% of those

There's a **Fine Line** between a **GROOVE** and a **RUT**

referrals into new clients would increase the customer base of the business unit by 10%.

I will let you calculate what a 10% increase in the number of clients over the next three to six months would do for your business.

To get your sales people started, try this.

At a future sales meeting, do a little role-playing. Have each of your representatives practice asking for referrals in front of the group. You can use the above example as a model, or you can create one of your own that may specifically fit your business.

The more your sales people practice asking for a referral, the more comfortable they will become doing this and the more often they will do it with their customers. Once the comfort level has been raised, I urge you to establish a referral program for your business. Then monitor the impact it has upon their performance and new customer development.

I know you will be pleasantly surprised at the increased — and positive — sales activity that occurs.

But what if you do not have a lot of customers to draw on? What if your business is relatively new? How can you get started?

As a new business owner, you can use a referral approach even if your customer base is limited. A recent experience I had offers a good example.

A few months ago, I had the opportunity to meet a young man who had started a business three months earlier. His business offered a specialized service and he

Chapter 5
Cold Calling is for Dummies

was anxious to contact midsize and large companies in his area to gain their interest and, hopefully, their business. He had prepared a direct mail letter, had a brochure, and had a list of 100 targeted companies. He was ready to go.

But I stopped him before he mailed off his precious cargo.

The good news was that he was planning to send each mailing to a specific individual at each targeted company. The bad news was that none of these individuals knew him.

His direct mail campaign was basically going to be a cold calling effort that, unfortunately, would gain him limited results.

So I recommended a slightly different approach. The approach I suggested to the young man is something I would like you to try, if you are in a similar position. And ask your sales people to try it, if you have a sales team.

I asked the young man to draw five circles on a piece of paper, each roughly three inches in diameter.

Then I asked him to write in each circle a name of a group of acquaintances that he knew. I offered a few ideas to get him started — groups like acquaintances at his church, school parents groups, the softball league he participated in, the volunteer organizations he belonged to, the association he joined, and his neighbors.

He quickly was able to label all five circles with the name of a group and added three more circles to complete his list.

There's a Fine Line between a GROOVE and a RUT

Next, I asked him to write in each circle the approximate number of acquaintances or friends he had in that identified group. Even he was surprised. The numbers averaged between 15 and 30.

We figured that the eight circles represented over 150 friendly contacts he could ask for help in connecting with the 100 companies he wanted to target.

As he began to communicate with his circles of friends, he was equally surprised to discover how many of them knew someone in a relatively important position in one or more of the 100 companies, or knew someone who did.

Using the mutual friend as a referral and initiating his network program, he was now armed with a contact name at most of his targeted companies.

Realizing that these contacts were unlikely to be a decision-makers for the services he was offering, I suggested that he restructure the letter slightly and ask if the contact would be kind enough to forward his information to the appropriate individual.

Although my suggestions created a lot more work for the young man and his new business, several positive results occurred.

Because he started with a mutual friend as a reference, his mailing was read when it was received.

Again, because of friendships and relationships, the receiving individual did pass the information on. And when the young man followed up by telephone, in many instances the contact helped him connect to the decision-maker.

It was hard to calculate how much more effective his mailing was versus a "cold call" mailing, but he is convinced today that the response he received more than justified the effort.

And, there was an added bonus.

A large number of his immediate friends and acquaintances now had become aware of his new enterprise and were helping to spread the good word.

Let me finish with a few very important points.

If someone provides you with a referral, be sure to ask permission to use his or her name when contacting that referral.

Sometimes the person you are asking to help you out may have additional information about the person they are referring you to that they may want to share. If possible, try to obtain as much additional information about the referral as possible (i.e., type of business, size, any particular aspects of the business that might lend itself to your product or service, and so on).

Immediate follow through is critical. The referral should be contacted within the next few working days. That's a must.

Finally, even if your efforts are unsuccessful, be sure to let your friend or acquaintance know the results of the referral call.

A lot of positives are created by asking others for referrals. This type of networking can broaden the friendships you have with non-business related contacts and they can create a stronger partner relationship with your business contacts that go beyond just transacting business.

In most instances, people like to be asked to help, give their opinions and offer advice. Not many people will turn down a sincere request for help, especially if it can improve someone's chances of being successful.

As you share these thoughts with your sales force, make them aware that referrals are a two-way street. Teach your representatives to learn as much as possible about the businesses their customers are in and what their needs are. The opportunity may arise where they and you can refer someone to their business.

I can't think of a better way to demonstrate good will and help your valued customers.

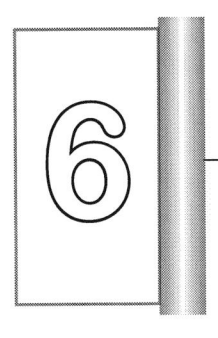

6 IT STARTS WITH GETTING THE APPOINTMENT

The very first obstacle that a salesperson must overcome is getting his or her "foot in the door." Creating that initial burst of interest from a potential client can be a daunting challenge.

In today's extremely busy business world, would-be buyers have little time to spend listening to sales presentations. Often their reaction to unsolicited calls is to ask that they be called next month (the "don't bother me now" response) or to send them something in the mail (which they likely will not read).

I have witnessed many salespeople get caught in this trap. They diligently call back time and time again to gain that elusive telephone audience and almost always fail. Or they put together a mail piece and send it off, only to find through a follow-up call that their recipient has not had time to look at it yet.

In both instances, a great deal of time and energy has been wasted with zero results.

There's a Fine Line between a GROOVE and a RUT

Unlike years ago, today there is an additional obstacle in trying to obtain an appointment. And it's a formidable opponent.

It's called ***voicemail*** and it has become the supreme blocking device for managing incoming telephone calls.

I recently did a short, unscientific test to see how impactful voicemail might be. I called 10 people, just to see if I could reach them with my first call.

Of the 10 calls, six sent me to voicemail. Three people were not there. I reached only one person.

One-out-of-ten is not a very attractive record.

And in real business situations, it would be highly unlikely that any of the six voicemail messages would ever be returned, unless the recipient had a very good reason to call me back.

Without a good reason in the prospect's mind to either take the call or to return it, salespeople will find it difficult to gain that all-important first appointment.

That is why the slide from a groove to a rut often starts with an increasing failure to obtain first-visit appointments. Failure to gain appointments equals failure to create potential new accounts which leads to declining new sales business.

As an employer or sales manager, you ***must*** monitor how effective each of your sales representatives is in this crucial area of professional selling.

If you discover that one of your sales reps is spending an increasing and possibly unjustified amount of time

Chapter 6
It Starts with Getting the Appointment

with current accounts and less time developing potential new clients, there may be a strong possibility that his or her ability to obtain first-visit appointments is declining. It's worth further investigation on your part.

And it all starts with getting that all-important appointment. Providing training in this vital area should be part of your ongoing sales training program.

Here's a great way to avoid a slump in the amount of new prospect appointments your sales people develop.

I am assuming that whether you are a business owner or manager, you attend and participate in your company's periodic sales meetings. If not, plan to take part in your next one.

When you arrive at the meeting, bring two phones with you. When it is your turn to participate, leave one phone by your chair, get up, walk around the room and hand the second phone to one of your sales representatives, one you have selected at random. Then walk back, sit down in your chair, and ask that representative to call you for an appointment.

No doubt you will have caught that sales representative off guard. What happens next will be very enlightening. It may surprise, amuse, disappoint, and possibly frustrate you.

You may even be delighted. But unless you have previously conducted training on how to successfully obtain telephone appointments, I doubt you will be.

However, if you carry this role-play exercise through to its entirety, you and your sales force will learn a great

There's a Fine Line between a GROOVE and a RUT

deal. And you will have performed a great service by improving the overall effectiveness of your sales force.

I have asked sales people, during sales training sessions, to call me for an appointment on a number of occasions. Let me share with you what happened the last time I did this.

After first recovering from shock and fear, the sales representative I had selected instinctively picked up the phone and started talking. Within a few moments the other meeting attendees noticed with amusement that I had not picked up my telephone.

When my representative had completed six or seven sentences, I stopped his presentation, had him observe that I was not holding my phone, and asked that he make a ringing sound so that I knew when to pick up the phone. This generated some laughter from the group.

My purpose was not to embarrass the representative. Instead it was designed to break any tension, relieve the anxiety, and make this role-playing exercise more fun. And it worked.

So my representative and I started over — this time with both phones raised — and the representative began again. His opening comments went something like this:

"Hello Mr. Kittredge, my name is Bill Hartman and I'm with ABC Products Company. We are one of the top manufacturers of widgets in the country and have been in business for over 40 years. Our goal is to help our customers improve their operating efficiencies. We have developed great expertise in improving production operations for our clients. I know we can do the same for you. Our widgets will help you reduce your costs, increase your profits, speed up your production time, strengthen your client relationships, enhance your corporate image, relieve your personal stress, improve your quality of life..."

On and on he went.

Finally, I stopped the representative again and ask him to start over for a third time.

And here is where I started the training program, introducing the most important rule when calling to obtain an appointment.

Fine Line
RULE # 6

In your very first statement, give the person you are calling a reason to **want** to talk with you.

Without a reason to talk to you, the person you are calling will most likely say that they are not interested, ask you to call at another time, or even hang up.

In your opening statements, you must make a connection with the person you are calling.

There's a Fine Line between a GROOVE and a RUT

How can you do that?

When I was first starting out as a sales representative, my manager told me that during any sales call, whether it be over the telephone or a face-to-face meeting, the very first thing I said would often determine whether that call would be successful or not.

So on day one, I began practicing the mechanics of my very first sentence and used it whether I was on the telephone or making a personal sales visit.

That practice paid off a short time later.

One week on the job, I remember making a personal sales call on a potential new prospect.

The person I was to meet greeted me in the lobby with the following opening.

"In three sentences or less, I would like you to tell me who you are and why you are here to see me."

If I had not practiced, I would have been just as shocked as that representative in the sales meeting. I took a deep breath and voiced the best three sentences I could think of. It worked, we connected and he invited me in.

So, can you make a connection with a prospect with the very first words you say? Yes, you can, as long as you say something that the prospect recognizes to be of value.

Let me repeat that. Your first sentences must say something that the prospect, not you, recognizes as being valuable.

Chapter 6
It Starts with Getting the Appointment

Stating that you're calling to save him money or save him time is really not that effective. First, it assumes something that has not been substantiated. Second, you don't know for sure if you can support the claim. And third, the value factor is too vague. It's not recognizable.

Some sales professionals have been trained to begin the conversation with a question rather than a statement. You've probably experienced this yourselves with some telemarketers.

"Ms. Jones, would you be interested if I could show you how to grow your investments at a rate greater than the market averages?"

"Mr. Peterson, what could your company do if it could lower its operating costs by 10 percent?"

Personally, I have never been an advocate of such lead questions and have never trained my sales people to use them. Such questions make assumptions that may or may not be true and, in general, sound flip and unprofessional.

I believe that there is a better way.

The best way to make a connection with your very first sentence is to mention either something that is, or someone who is, recognizable to the person you are talking with.

Do you remember Fine Line Rule #5 in the last chapter? It stated that a current customer would be receptive to giving you a referral if you asked them for one. Using these referrals in your opening statements is an effective way to obtain appointments.

There's a Fine Line between a GROOVE and a RUT

If you mention the name of someone both you and your prospect know — and trust — and connect that name to a benefit, your chances of attracting interest rise exponentially.

Here's an example of an effective opening statement.

"Mr. Roberts, my name is George Kittredge. Harold Butler, at ABC Company, gave me your name and telephone number and suggested I call you. If you have just a moment, I'd like to tell you why he asked me to call you."

Short and to the point. Here's how the mechanics of such a three-sentence statement work.

The first sentence introduces me by name. Notice I did not mention my company's name. It's not necessary at this point.

The second sentence identifies a mutual acquaintance who is trying to connect the two of us. Assuming that the acquaintance is someone my prospect respects (highly likely), the chances are good that he will at least listen to the next thing I say.

The last sentence serves two purposes. It basically asks for permission for me to explain the purpose of my call and tells the person I am calling that I will get right to the point.

Such a three-sentence opening statement is short, powerful, polite and professional.

It's an opening that does not require you to memorize anything or to have a text for you to read. And

Chapter 6
It Starts with Getting the Appointment

it makes it difficult for the person you are calling to say that he is not interested.

This type of opening statement is also easy for your sales force to practice and master.

In your sales meeting, after you have discussed with your group this three-sentence opening statement, ask the representative you first selected to call you again to try such a statement on you.

Notice the confidence and lack of hesitancy in your representative's voice. I'll bet it is much improved over his or her first attempt.

Now go around the room and have each person practice such an opening statement.

It is so simple that it may seem ridiculous. But the mere fact that very few sales people use such an opening statement suggests it does need to be practiced.

"Ms. Briggs, my name is George Kittredge. Susan Parker at The Learning Center gave me your name and number and suggested I call you. If you have just a minute, I'd like to tell you why she asked me to call you."

Pretty easy, isn't it?

I cannot guarantee that it will gain you an interested audience every time, but I can guarantee that it will generate a much higher rate of interest than non-referral calls. There's less of a chance that your prospect will cut you off before he or she has heard the major purpose of your call.

A couple of additional points.

There's a Fine Line between a GROOVE and a RUT

I prefer such a short opening statement because it allows the person I am calling to respond. In essence, it begins a dialog.

There is always the possibility that my prospect may not be interested in continuing the conversation. I have given them the opportunity to either continue or terminate the call. If they wish to end the call, despite my use of a referral, I would be better off knowing that in the beginning rather that at the end of the conversation.

In almost every instance when I have used the referral connection, however, the person I have called has given me time to explain my purpose or, if that moment was inconvenient for them, scheduled a firm time for me to call back.

An opening statement I do not use and do not train sales people to use is to begin the telephone conversation with something like, "Hello Mr. Goodman. How are you today?"

This is not the time for one of those, "How are you. I am fine," conversations we've been learning to avoid.

That kind of opening serves no useful purpose whatsoever. It presents a question that neither one of you is interested in hearing the answer to and does nothing to promote a constructive dialog. In fact, a how are you question coming from an unannounced stranger can create a mental red flag in the prospect's mind and immediately put them on the defensive.

So I suggest you eliminate the how-are-you question from your telephone presentation.

Chapter 6
It Starts with Getting the Appointment

Okay, so we've established that using a referral works as a way to get in the door. What if you don't have a referral? Is there anything else you can do to create that initial interest with a prospect you wish to make contact with?

Yes, there is.

My suggestion is to use a ***reference connection***, as compared to a referral connection.

Let's assume that I would like an appointment with the person in charge of materials management at a company I have identified as a potential client. Rather than attempt to contact that person in my initial call to the company, I first call someone else. It could be anyone in the human resource area, or marketing, or production, or operations.

Most importantly, I try to establish contact with someone above an entry-level position.

The purpose of my initial call is purely fact-finding. I want to find out the name of the person in charge of materials management and confirm, as best I can, that this person is the correct person for me to call.

Usually this requires a brief explanation of what my company or I do and the types of people we work with at other companies. Then I ask if the person in charge of their materials management would be the person I should contact and who that person is.

Once I obtain the name of the person I should call, I also obtain the name of the person I am currently talking to and thank them for their help.

65

Now I am prepared to make my actual sales call.

My opening statement is slightly different from my referral call. It goes something like this:

"Mr. Williams, my name is George Kittredge. I was just speaking with Patricia Roberts in your production office and she felt you would be the best person for me to talk with. If you have just a moment, I'd like to tell you the purpose of my call."

Although the referral opening and reference opening are very similar, you can see the subtle difference.

In both, I introduce myself, mention a name that should be recognized by the person I am calling, and state that if they will allow me to, I would like to tell them my reason for contacting them.

The referral connection implies that the third party referred me to my prospect. The reference connection explains how I learned who I should call.

Both opening statements can accomplish your first objective: to gain a receptive ear to hear the purpose of your call.

Then, when your prospect gives you permission to explain the reason for your call, you must be ready.

When using a referral, I briefly explain (1) the relationship I have with our common acquaintance, (2) the benefits he or she has received from using my products and services, (3) how our common acquaintance felt similar benefits could be realized by my prospect, and (4) that I would like to make an appointment to share this information in more detail.

Chapter 6
It Starts with Getting the Appointment

If I have presented something my prospect believes may be of immediate value, I will obtain the appointment.

When using a reference, my explanation is slightly different. In this instance I usually relate any benefits mentioned to businesses or operations that may be in a similar line of work or have similar customer bases as my prospect. I suggest that such benefits could be possible for my prospect and ask for the appointment.

It's a more difficult challenge, but is successful more times than not.

I can't stress the following enough.

The key to gaining that first appointment with a prospect is research. Have your salespeople learn as much as they can about their prospects, particularly information that relates to any products or services you offer, before they make that call. websites offer good information. And both your referral and reference people may be valuable resources as well.

Yes, researching is time consuming, but it's much more effective than just picking up the telephone and cold calling. Remember, cold calling is for dummies!

There's a Fine Line between a GROOVE and a RUT

7 THE SELLING AGENDA

Can you recall the best sales presentation ever given to you? A presentation made to you by a sales professional who stands out above all the others? If so, what made it so special, and what do you remember most about it?

Now picture those qualities in your sales force.

Although it was more than ten years ago, I can clearly remember the best sales presentation made to me. I was in a senior management position, and a woman in her middle to late forties came to see me in my office.

She was a representative for a national publishing company that published and marketed executive summaries. Their topics ranged from summaries of lengthy business reports and business books to fiction and historical novels. Her products were designed for people with limited time to read the more detailed information or complete works.

There's a Fine Line between a GROOVE and a RUT

Prior to her visit, she had called to obtain the appointment referencing two business colleagues I knew as current subscribers to her products.

I have never before or after seen anyone as cordial, polite, businesslike, and professional as she. She knew her products inside and out and provided sufficient documentation for the claims she was making on behalf of them.

When she arrived, she started by giving me a brief outline of what our meeting would entail. It would last no longer than 30 minutes, and she told me what I could expect from her during that time. Basically she laid out a roadmap of the things we would talk about.

Her outline completed, she then provided me with background information about herself and her company. She asked pertinent questions regarding what I enjoyed reading, both for business and pleasure, and queried me about my time constraints.

She listed product benefits, showed examples, offered testimonials, and closed with a no-risk guarantee. Her delivery was both to the point and conversational. Her confidence and ability were easy to recognize.

I was impressed.

Why? Because she was a professional demonstrating what I call the selling agenda.

She obviously had pre-planned our meeting and had outlined in her mind, as well as in her notes (which she

Chapter 7
The Selling Agenda

would occasionally refer to), the information she wanted to learn from me and the key points she wanted to make.

I found out later that she was the top sales professional in her national company. She was very successful. A consistent performer, in her groove.

No wonder.

There have been a number of studies done regarding selling success. Some studies indicate that as few as four percent of people who are in sales realize financial independence at the end of their careers.

Whether it's four, six, or eight percent, that's a very low number. And when you consider the number of people who have been and are in sales, the statistics are even more impressive. Why do you think this is?

I believe that the vast majority of sales people do not achieve true sales success (i.e. financial independence) because they are not that good at selling and they don't know why.

Here's the primary reason: they lack the skills in sales techniques that are so crucial to achieving positive results. And they fail to keep studying the profession. They fail to keep learning no matter what level of success they are having.

I have seen many sales professionals who, at the start of their careers, performed extremely well. Always at the top of the monthly quota chart, leaders in new account development, knowledgeable about their products, and services and well organized.

There's a Fine Line between a GROOVE and a RUT

But as the years went by, their sales performance began to wane. They moved from the top of the class, to mediocrity, and finally into the lower echelon.

What happened to them?

In all too many cases, the answer is failure to learn new methods. Or more accurately, lack of continued training. What started out as successful selling eventually developed into selling the same old way year in and year out, regardless of whether the success was there or not. These people knew only one way to sell and failed to make the effort to learn new skills and try new approaches.

Do not let this happen to your sales force.

In order to sustain sales success, your sales force must continue to learn and develop new and additional selling skills.

What happens if new skills are not learned?

As old skills become less effective (due to cultural, economic, technological, and/or competitive pressures), there is a tendency to stop using those techniques and rely on other skills that still seem to work.

If your sales people are not learning and employing new ideas, their portfolio of skills atrophies. The skills they continue to use become fewer and fewer. Until finally they know only how to sell one way. They have now crossed over that fine line. Where once they were in a selling groove, they now are in a rut.

For example, how many sales people do you know that sell only through relationship building? In other words, their customers are their "buddies," buying

Chapter 7
The Selling Agenda

from them because they are long-time friends. They arrive with donuts and spend time talking about family and recreational activities rather than what's really important to creating a growing business relationship.

These sales representatives are comfortable calling on their old accounts, have difficulty creating new business clients and tend to give lip service to any accounts they inherit. Although developing a friendly relationship with your customers is an important aspect, it is just one part of a successful, growing business partnership.

Then you have the other end of the spectrum.

Some sales representatives do not consistently use any selling skills. This is called "winging it."

He or she arrives at the customer's premises with very little idea as to what is to take place, but figures that during the conversation, something will occur to make the sale. If you've ever traveled with a rep that wings it, you'll notice that every call is different — totally different. But the results may be the same — lots of time spent and few sales.

One of the most positive things you can do for your sales force, including your veteran players, something that you can do for that new hire you have just made, and a vital step for the future success of your business, is to teach all of them how to use your "selling agenda."

You notice that I said *your* selling agenda, not mine. It's not difficult for you to teach them your agenda, and the results will be dramatic.

So what is a selling agenda?

73

There's a **Fine Line** between a **GROOVE** and a **RUT**

When you visit a McDonald's® restaurant, do you know what's going to happen? Of course, you do. You have an excellent idea of what the quality of the food will be, what it looks and tastes like, and what the inside of the establishment will look like.

In one McDonald's after another, you expect your experience to be the same. The burgers look and taste the same no matter where you go. No surprises. And that's what brings you back time and time again (if you like the fast food at McDonald's).

That's one example of a selling agenda. The people who work at McDonald's are trained in the McDonald's style. The owners of the franchises are trained first at McDonald's "Hamburger University" near Chicago. Although they each have their own personalities, the mechanics of what they do are based upon a specific agenda that they are trained to perform.

There are tens of thousands of successful franchises throughout the United States and the main factor in their success is the execution of the selling agenda.

> **Fine Line**
> **RULE # 7**
>
> If you want your sales organization to perform at the top of its game and present the best possible image of your company, teach them <u>your</u> selling agenda.

Chapter 7
The Selling Agenda

Teach them your company's selling style. They will certainly add their own personality to what they learn, and that is what you want them to do. But you need to provide them with a basic agenda.

Here is how you can do it.

As a first step, think about what you would like each of your representatives to accomplish (besides closing a sale) on each sales call that they make. The operative phrase here is "on each sales call they make." The list you generate is the beginning of your agenda.

As an example, let me suggest the following as a possible agenda outline — again, it's a list of objectives you would like your sales representatives to accomplish on each call.

1. Establish credibility for your company and the sales rep and start building a trust relationship between your company and the prospect.

2. Learn about the prospect's business and objectives.

3. Identify specific priority needs where your products or services might benefit the prospect.

4. Make a complete sales presentation for one or more of your products or services.

5. If calling on a current customer, ask for a testimonial citing the benefits they have received from your products and services.

6. If calling on a current customer, ask them for two or more names of others that they would suggest you contact.

7. Create a reason for a follow-up call and schedule it.

There's a Fine Line between a GROOVE and a RUT

The above list is just a start. You may think of other specific objectives you would like to include. Feel free to add or change anything on this list.

If you have just launched a new product or service, you might want each representative to introduce the new item on each call. If you are conducting market research, you might want your representatives to be part of the information gathering.

The important point is that the agenda you create is something you want your sales organization to use on every sales call they make.

In addition, as you prepare to discuss creating a selling agenda with your sales force and ask for their input, having some idea of what your agenda looks like will be helpful in stimulating their ideas.

How many of your sales people use a selling agenda like this in their face-to-face meetings with your clients and prospects? If your answer is less than all of them, you have a wonderful opportunity for a sales training exercise that will pay dividends for them and for your company.

If you don't currently have a selling agenda in place, enlist your own sales force to help you develop one. Make it an objective in an upcoming sales meeting to establish a selling agenda for your company. You can start by telling them what you would like to accomplish.

1. That you would like to create a selling agenda, or a short list of objectives that you would like to see each representative accomplish on each of his or her sales calls.

Chapter 7
The Selling Agenda

2. That the purpose of creating this agenda is to help them maximize the effectiveness of the time they spend with their clients and prospects.

3. That this agenda will serve only as a basis for discussion with clients and in no way inhibit the creativity and personality that they bring to their client relationships.

4. That you would like them, working together with you, to create an agenda that they feel best accomplishes these goals.

Then, share with them your vision of an agenda outline, perhaps similar to the seven objectives I listed above. Ask for their input and recommendations for any changes or additions they would like to see. Once this list is agreed upon, you and your sales team are ready to develop the agenda in more detail.

There's a Fine Line between a GROOVE and a RUT

8. ESTABLISHING CREDIBILITY

No profitable business relationship can be created or maintained unless there is mutual trust and respect from both parties.

Therefore, establishing your and your company's credibility with your audience is an excellent place to begin your selling agenda.

Ask your sales people to list what they believe are the best examples that demonstrate your company's philosophy of putting your clients' well-being at the top of your priority list. What are the best examples all of you can collectively think of that show your sincere desire to put your clients' needs first? I call these examples "credibility builders."

Could it be the length of time your customers have been using your products and services?

Is it your reputation for customer service?

Perhaps it is the high marks your company received from a recent business survey.

There's a Fine Line between a GROOVE and a RUT

It might be some public recognition you received.

Is it the credentials of the key people that work for your company?

Or is it your company's in-depth experience and knowledge in a particular business area?

As each idea comes forth, write it down. When you feel that the list is fairly complete, have the group discuss each idea. Determine how you can visually support each claim you make.

This support might be through customer letters or comments you have received. It may be from articles that have been written about your company. It might be an award you received.

When you have completed your discussion, ask your sales group to select at least three credibility builders they believe best represent the company. Develop some supporting documents that can be shown to prospects and current customers and ask your salespeople to begin using them in their presentations.

Let's assume your company provides financial services to other businesses. Let's further assume that, after you have identified and discussed with your salespeople a list of credibility builders, they decide on the following three specific examples to include in their presentations.

1. Growth in the number of clients and businesses over the last two years (you will need to provide them with accurate numbers and statistics).

2. Receipt of a recognition award the company earned earlier in the year for outstanding professional achievement (you will need to provide them with the article or similar documentation that identifies and explains the award).

3. Professional experience of the company staff (you will need to provide biographical information on key players, noting achievements and experience).

In a follow-up sales meeting, with supporting documents available, schedule time for each sales representative to role-play. Ask each participant to present your company's credibility builders to the rest of the group as if they were talking with their client or prospect. Continue the practice session until each can speak clearly, succinctly and with confidence.

Here is an example of how someone might present his or her credibility builders to a prospect or current customer:

"Mr. Client, as we begin I would like to share some information about my company with you to help you gain a better picture of who we are and what we do. This chart will give you an idea of how we have grown over the last two years. The number of businesses we work with has more than doubled and our overall business has tripled during this time. We believe these statistics offer good examples of the mutually beneficial relationships we have developed with our clients.

"Six months ago our company was recognized by the Business Consulting Organization of America for our expertise in solving financial business problems. This article appeared in our local newspaper as well as in the association's national magazine. We are proud of this recognition and use it as a benchmark for our continued work with our clients.

"And finally, here is some information about the key players in our company. These are the individuals who would be working with you. I will leave with you information about their qualifications, experience, and areas of expertise.

"We believe our resources and skills are second to none and hope you will give us the opportunity to work with you."

That's pretty powerful stuff and a great beginning to a sales presentation. How many of your salespeople begin their presentations with something like that?

Fine Line
RULE # 8

A successful customer relationship begins by establishing your credibility with your business prospect.

If your sales organization is not sharing your credibility builders with their clients, then they — and you — are missing a great opportunity.

Such information will give your clients and prospects a better understanding of who you are and the value you can bring to the relationship.

It strengthens the trust in the relationships with your clients and will likely increase the probability of the number of prospects who will say "yes" to your proposals and recommendations.

I urge you to make establishing credibility a part of your selling agenda to both current and potential new customers.

There's a Fine Line between a GROOVE and a RUT

9 THE SALES PRESENTATION

As your customers learn about you, it is equally important that you learn about them.

Very often salespeople are in such a rush to share all the wonderful things their products and services will do for their customer, they tend to skip right by the part where they need to listen and learn some basic information about who they are talking with.

Smart salespeople do their homework and learn as much as possible about the client or prospect prior to making the sales call. Researching the prospect's website, obtaining literature about the business, and reviewing other resources provide a great deal of information.

Some people believe that asking general questions to someone about their company shows ignorance or lack of preparation. However, I do not agree. Getting the prospect to share some information about his or her business should definitely be part of your selling agenda.

Why?

Chances are that even if you have done research on your client's business, they will offer some additional information that you may not have discovered. Also, people enjoy talking about what they do, what their company does, their challenges and expectations. Asking pertinent questions is an excellent way for your sales people to create a dialogue with their prospects and avoid the conversation becoming a one-way exercise.

Finally, questions can demonstrate your sincerity in wanting to learn about their business and keeping their best interests in mind. And you must be sincere.

So now we have another valuable exercise for you and your salespeople to do during one of your sale meetings.

Ask your sales force to help you develop a short list of questions that each of them can use during sales calls. Some people refer to these as "probing" questions. However, I don't like that term. It sounds as if you are doing undercover work searching for corporate secrets.

I prefer to call them informational questions, for that is exactly what they are. They are merely questions designed to allow you to gather information that will make your comments and presentations more meaningful.

And remember, the best questions are open-ended questions that require more than a yes or no answer. Here are some possible examples.

1. "Mr. Customer, what do you like best about the (product or service) you are currently using?"

2. "If you could make them today, what changes would you like to see made?"

3. "Over the last two years, in what areas have you increased the amount of services you outsource?"

4. "What would you say are your top three priorities regarding this project?"

5. "What will be your decision-making process?"

6. "What type of timeline have you established?"

The list of informational questions should be a short list. What's important here is that the answers to your questions provide you and your sales force with important insights about your prospect's needs and objectives, and that the information you discover relates to the products or services you are offering.

Quite likely, the responses to each informational question will lead to a series of clarifying questions. They also should provide some direction as to how to position your proposals and offerings.

There is another important benefit you will receive from having your sales reps ask similar questions to their clients and prospects.

If you take the time (and I urge that you do) to analyze the data gathered by your sales force, the collective information obtained from your many customers and prospects can provide valuable insights that will help you develop sound future marketing strategies.

It is very important that once you have developed a short list of questions, you provide your salespeople with a written list of these questions. A list they can take with them and refer to during their sales calls.

It is extremely difficult, if not impossible, to remember everything you wish to accomplish on a sales call and to complete these items in an orderly and timely fashion.

I have always taught my salespeople to bring notes with them and to take notes during the sales conversations. I remember what a college professor once told me. When you write something down, you don't have to remember it. The only thing you have to remember is where you wrote it down.

The key to a successful sales presentation lies in identifying the need in the listener's mind. This is why informational questions are so important. If your sales representative launches into a presentation without identifying a need that your product or service addresses, most of his or her efforts will be wasted.

In Chapter Four we discussed using features, advantages, and benefits as the best way to tell your business story. I'm convinced that every presentation your sales representatives make should include FABs about the products and services they are promoting and the company that they work for.

And each set of FABs should relate directly to an identified need or objective previously expressed by your listener.

Let me give you an example.

Let's assume that your company develops automated customer service programs for your clients. During your informational questioning with Mr. Ross, a prospect,

Chapter 9
The Sales Presentation

you discover that one of his objectives is to ensure that each of his customers receives a followup contact within two weeks after receiving an order.

Using the features, advantages, benefits approach, you might present your program in the following manner:

> You: "Mr. Ross, you mentioned earlier your desire to better ensure a two-week follow-up with customers after they have received an order from your company, is that correct?"
>
> Mr. Ross: "Yes it is."
>
> You: "One of the features of our customer service package is the automated follow-up alert system built into the program. Here's how it works. Upon shipment to your customer, the system will automatically alert the salesperson of record and any management people you authorize when a follow-up contact should be made. You can determine the time frame, whether one week, ten days, two weeks, whatever is appropriate. If the follow-up contact is not made within the prescribed time, e-mails are sent daily to remind those individuals that the follow-up task has not been completed."
>
> You continue: "As a result, no customer follow-up can be overlooked or missed. And as an additional benefit, you and the managers you authorize can access the follow-up data base at any time to learn the status of each follow-up currently scheduled. This system

has proven to be a great benefit to our clients and I am confident that it would fulfill your follow-up objectives. What do you think?"

Bang! You've just hit the nail on the head. You discovered an objective, responded with a feature/advantage/benefit solution, and asked for agreement. You are one step closer to gaining a new customer.

Making your sales presentation a series of features, advantages, and benefits is an extremely effective way of promoting your products and services. Using FABs in your sales presentations will definitely increase your probability of selling success. Give it a try.

10 THE POWER OF TESTIMONIALS

What's the best way you can support the features, advantages, and benefits you're claiming in your sales presentations?

The answer, in one word is: ***testimonials***.

Whether verbal or written, testimonials pack a wallop.

Imagine your sales representative backing up a FAB statement with:

"Mr. Ross, I brought along a copy of this letter, written by the VP of Marketing for ABC Company. They installed our follow-up alert system over a year ago, and I'd like to read to you what he said about the system and what it did for their repeat business."

What impact do you think that kind of statement would have on your prospect? On your sales person's confidence level?

Right now, think about how many testimonials you have equipped your sales force with. How well do they

There's a Fine Line between a GROOVE and a RUT

tie into your products' benefits? How effectively do your sales people use them?

Do they use them at all?

If your answers are not enough, not sure, or no, I urge you to begin building a testimonial file for all of your sales representatives to use. Then put testimonials to work for you. It is relatively easy to do and it is your salespeople who can create such a file for you.

I would be a very rich man if I received a dollar for each time a sales representative left a sales call with a satisfied customer, but did not ask for a testimonial.

The importance of testimonials cannot be overstated. Yet, in the vast majority of situations, salespeople forget all about obtaining them.

Why? Because it has not been made part of their selling agenda. If it were, your sales people would be loaded with testimonials — testimonials from satisfied clients that could be used in future sales presentations, as well as in the literature that you distribute and on your Website.

I have also seen testimonials used effectively in tradeshow and advertising displays.

Again, the importance of testimonials cannot be overstated, but you have to obtain them first. How? Your sales team can make it happen.

And so, here is Fine Line Rule Number Nine.

Chapter 10
The Power of Testimonials

Fine Line
RULE # 9

> Customer testimonials are powerful selling tools that are easy to obtain. Just **ask** for them.

Here is how easy it can be to obtain a testimonial.

Assume that one of your sales representatives is completing a personal sales call on one of your longtime customers. She finishes the call with the following:

Sales rep: "Ms. Harrison, you have been using our service for almost three years now. Is that correct?"

Ms. Harrison: "Yes, I believe it is."

Sales rep: "What would you say is the greatest benefit you have received from this service?"

Ms. Harrison: "Let's see. I would say that the greatest benefit for me is the peace of mind I have in knowing that I have experienced professionals using the latest technology and doing this job far better than my staff or I could do with our resources. Your work has always been complete, on time, accurate and cost-effective."

> Sales rep: "That's a wonderful statement, Ms. Harrison. I am currently talking to several business owners who would love to hear your comments. Would it be possible for you to provide me with a written testimonial that I could share with them? I would be very appreciative."

Or,

> Sales rep: "That's a wonderful statement, Ms. Harrison. I am currently talking to several business owners who are evaluating a similar system. Would you mind if I shared your remarks with them?"

It's just that easy to ask for a testimonial, either written or verbal.

There will be some situations where your customer's company may have a policy against providing written testimonials, or confidentiality may preclude something in writing. However, in most instances your clients will be pleased to grant your representatives a testimonial.

The key is to ask for them.

I urge you to train your staff to solicit testimonials whenever and wherever they can. Make it part of your selling agenda. Make it a part of every sales call. You will be astounded at the results.

And be prepared to show your sales team how to and when to effectively use testimonials in a verbal presentation. Don't overlook the value of incorporating testimonials into your written material, as well.

Chapter 10
The Power of Testimonials

Role-play during sales meetings until each member of your sales team is comfortable about asking for testimonials. Then, at subsequent sales meetings, have each representative share the testimonials he or she has obtained. These are testimonials that everyone can use. Your sales people will benefit, and your business will benefit also.

The same reasoning holds true for referrals, as well. When your sales people are not asking for a testimonial, they should be asking for a referral. They should be asking for someone who their customer would suggest they contact.

If you need to, please re-read Chapter Five. It's a proven fact that the use of referrals is the most effective way for your salespeople to be invited to meet with a potential new client.

And once they are in front of their prospects, it is a proven fact that the use of testimonials is the most effective way of proving your benefit statements.

There's a Fine Line between a GROOVE and a RUT

11
CREATING A REASON TO COME BACK

There is another aspect of an effective sales call that is overlooked more often than not. It's the failure to create a reason to make a return sales call.

If you want to test this theory, spend a few days making joint sales calls with your sales people. Keep track of how many, prior to ending a sales call, establish a reason to come back. If you come up with 20 percent or more, you're beating the averages.

I recall one sales representative who worked for me who never established a reason to return on any of his sales calls. Even when he obtained an order, he never asked for a follow-up call.

One of the most intriguing things about Jim was his fear of prolonging a sales call after he had made the sale. It was kind of like, "Thank you for the order. Have a nice day. Goodbye."

After observing this on a number of joint sales calls, I asked him why he was in such a rush to "get out of there." His answer surprised me.

There's a Fine Line between a GROOVE and a RUT

He told me that he feared that if he stayed to talk about anything else, the customer might change his mind regarding the order he had just placed and take back the order. He felt that if he left quickly with the order, the order was "safe."

I learned this the first day I traveled with him. And he was a pretty good sales representative, too. He was achieving or exceeding his sales quota on a regular basis, knew his product line, and presented himself well. His fear was certainly unfounded.

He hadn't crossed over that fine line yet – and I was determined not to let him get close to it.

I explained to Jim that developing a solid business relationship with his customers was something that evolved through a series of "connected" sales calls. Even though he knew he planned to call on that customer again, his customer might not realize it.

Because his relationship with this customer was something that he valued, it was important that he convey his desire to, at a later date, share additional information in an effort to provide further benefits to the customer.

There was also an additional benefit to Jim that he was overlooking.

By not establishing a return date, Jim would have to spend additional amount of time in the future calling to set up a follow-up appointment. We all know how long it can sometimes take to connect with someone by telephone. Between voicemails and callbacks, it can be a week or more.

Chapter 11
Creating a Reason to Come Back

Why not spend just a minute prior to completing the sales visit by setting up the next meeting?

Sometimes establishing a reason to call back is as easy as needing to follow-up to evaluate the results of whatever product or service was purchased.

"Mr. Rodgers, the new equipment you have ordered will be delivered on the 13th and should be up and running within 48 hours. I'd like to return on the 17th to check on the installation and obtain your comments as to its initial performance. Would you be available at 10 a.m. to meet with me?"

Sometimes a reason to make a follow-up call is to share something new with the client that, based upon your observations, might be of benefit.

"Mr. Rodgers, we unfortunately did not have time this morning to discuss all the information I wanted to share with you. We have just introduced a new software upgrade that I believe can enhance the performance of your equipment. Would you be available Tuesday morning, the 12th, to meet with me? I will bring a ten-minute demonstration module that will show you exactly how the new software works."

The bottom line here is that an important part of the sales call agenda includes scheduling a follow-up call. It may mean scheduling a return visit within a few days, or a week, or a month. But make sure your sales people get the follow-up on their schedule.

Notice also that in the examples above, the sales person was very specific about the time and date of the next meeting. The client may suggest other times, but it's up to the sales person to ask initially and offer the time and date.

Not only does it save your sales representatives the time and effort it would take to later call for an appointment, but it creates that series of connected sales calls that bring continuity and a "working together" atmosphere to the business relationship.

Establishing a reason to come back is a critical part of the selling agenda.

12 HOW TO ASK THE BIG QUESTION

There you have it, the selling agenda that I have used personally and trained others to use for many years:

1. Establish credibility.

2. Learn about your prospect's business.

3. Identify key needs and objectives.

4. Present your products and services using features, advantages, and benefits and provide support for your FABs with testimonials.

5. Ask for testimonials.

6. Ask for referrals.

7. Establish a reason to come back.

This selling agenda has worked for me. And your selling agenda, once you have developed it, will work for you.

But there is one other item that is on my agenda and needs to be on yours. And it should be placed right after item number four on the above list.

Perhaps you know what it is.

> **Fine Line**
> **RULE # 10**
>
> Ask for the order.

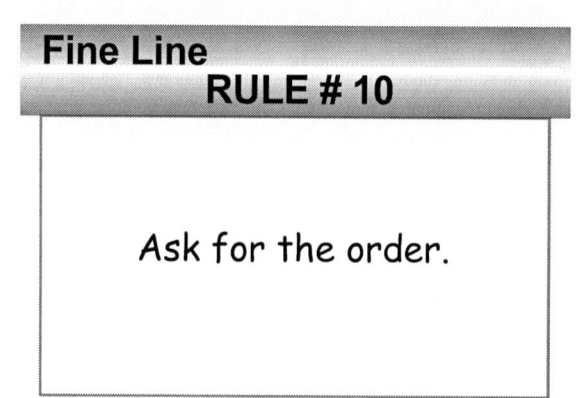

Have you ever experienced a time when you have been in the middle of your sales presentation and your listener interrupted you with, "Stop. I've heard enough. I'm sold. Where do I sign?"

What a wonderful thought. If only it were that easy.

In my sales career, such an interruption has not happened very often. Like most sales professionals, I almost always have to ask for the order.

Truth is, if you want to get the order, you must ask for it. If you want to hit the ball, you are going to have to swing at it.

Asking for an order, for some, can be the most difficult aspect of the selling agenda. The perception of rejection can be high. I've met some sales representatives who were very reluctant to ask for the order, even when they had

Chapter 12
How to Ask the Big Question

completed an excellent sales presentation. Their fear of a "no" answer was just too great. To them, asking the big question became a very uncomfortable part of the meeting.

Is there a way to ask for the order without creating anxiety or fear? Is there a way to comfortably ask your audience to buy from you?

Yes, there is. That's what this chapter is all about.

As a business owner or sales manager, asking for an order may be second nature to you. It may simply be the natural progression of a sales call and discussion and something that, over the years, you have become comfortable in doing.

But it is likely that some of your sales representatives may not feel the same way. In fact, over the years I've met and worked with a significant number of sales representatives who are hesitant to ask for an order.

This is what some of them have told me.

Their biggest fear in asking for the order is rejection. A "no" answer. Once a no is given, they believe there is a high potential that all may be lost. That to change that negative response into a positive one is almost impossible.

Strangely enough, many of those sales professionals believed that by not asking for the order, the opportunity for making the sale would always remain possible. That if they continued to make repeated calls on the prospect, they hoped that the prospect would eventually buy their product or service.

I have only had one representative on any of my sales staffs where that strategy worked. Bob was a unique individual and one of the hardest workers I ever met. He would continue to call on his prospect until he got a yes answer. I was so intrigued by his methods that I asked several of his customers why they bought from him. Their answers were all the same.

"It was the only way I could get him to stop calling on me for a while."

Rather fascinating, isn't it?

But for the hundreds of other sales representatives I've worked with, the "keep calling on them" strategy failed.

If your sales team submits sales reports, there are things you might spot that may indicate not asking for the order. Look for comments such as "contact next week for decision" or "prospect hasn't had a chance to complete evaluation of proposal." When such remarks are repeated over and over, chances are high that your representative is not effectively asking your prospect to become your customer.

If that is indeed the case, I offer this suggestion.

During one of your sales meetings, ask each of the attendees to give you a closing statement they use. Write each statement down on a blackboard or easel. Then have the group discuss and evaluate each statement for its effectiveness. Some statements may be very professional and effective. Others will probably be weak.

Statements such as "Would you like the red one or the blue one?" or "Would you prefer to start the program next Monday or Tuesday?" really don't work that well.

So what does work?

Chapter 12
How to Ask the Big Question

There are simple closing statements that can be used effectively in a non-confrontational, yet professional manner. There is one, in particular, that I like very much.

A number of years ago, a sales colleague I was teamed up with introduced me to a closing statement he used all the time. We were selling new technology equipment to the printing industry and calling on some of the largest high-speed printers in the country. Our goal was to establish a one-year program with each prospect, but the economics allowed us to accept a six-month commitment if necessary.

My colleague said he always kept his special closing statement "in his back pocket," to be used when he really needed it. I began using that same statement shortly thereafter and found it to be the most effective way to elicit a positive response from my audience.

It is a statement I have been able to adapt to any kind of business, product, or service. I'm going to share it with you and suggest that you teach your sales force to use it, or develop something similar.

Let's assume that you sell a Website service to small businesses and that you have just completed your sales presentation to Mr. Blackwell, a small business owner. You've asked all the necessary questions about his needs and obtained the answers you sought. You've pointed out all the appropriate features, advantages, and benefits. You supported those benefits with documented testimonials.

You've received positive responses and agreement from your listener throughout your discussions. And you

There's a Fine Line between a GROOVE and a RUT

now believe that Mr. Blackwell has all the information he needs to make a positive business decision.

Here is an example of what you can say next to close your summation and ask for the order.

"Mr. Blackwell what other clients have done when they have reached the same point in decision-making that you are at right now, is to ask us to let them test our service for a six-month period. They have found that this amount of time has allowed them to make a complete and informed decision on establishing a longer program. And this is what I would like to suggest we do now!"

It is just that simple. And it's very effective.

Notice that my closing comment is **not** a question, but rather a statement. It's a statement, however, that calls for a reaction. When I used this closing statement, more often than not my prospect responded positively.

Regardless of the type of business you are in, whether you provide products or services, you can modify and use this statement to fit your particular situation.

Your company, no doubt, has a money-back satisfaction guarantee on anything and everything your customers buy from you. If you don't, you need to put one in writing and make sure your representatives tell your customers.

Stop and think about it. Whether stated or not, any time a customer buys something from you for the first time, it is a trial order. They are trying it out to see if they want to continue to use it.

Chapter 12
How to Ask the Big Question

This is why my colleague's closing statement made so much sense. What a comfortable way to begin a trial program with a new client.

I urge you to share such a statement with your sales force. Have them memorize it and practice it during your sales meeting sessions.

Yes, this is something they do need to memorize.

And have them put it in their back pocket, ready to be used when they need it. You will have done them a great service.

"What others have done when they have reached the same point in decision-making that you are at right now, is to try (test) the product (service) for a three (six) month period to fully evaluate the results. And that is what I suggest we do now!"

Your sales representatives will never again be fearful of asking for a decision from any of their prospects and they will never again have to struggle to find the right words to say to obtain that decision.

But let's say that even after your sales representative has made an excellent closing statement and asked for the order, he or she gets a response of, "Let me think about it. I'll call you next week."

What should your representative do now?

When asking someone to make a decision, many people believe that there is only one of two answers they will hear.

A "yes" or a "no."

However, there is a third answer that is probably the most common response of all. And sometimes, no matter how well you have presented yourself, you get that third response – the "no decision at all" response.

Indecision from a prospective customer can be one of the most difficult obstacles to overcome, and it is very likely the most common obstacle your salespeople face. In the prospect's mind, indecision avoids a perceived risk in trying something new. Indecision eliminates a perceived awkward or confrontational situation. Indecision eliminates the need to make a decision right now.

Indecision has a lot going for it, but none of it is positive for your sales representative.

Unfortunately, many salespeople treat indecision as an acceptable response. But they really shouldn't.

Indecision means that they haven't really sold their prospects on whatever it is that they are selling. That there is something missing in the equation. That an important objection has not been properly addressed. Their work is not done.

I have witnessed salespeople accepting indecision as the end of the sales call, then make repeated sales visits and telephone calls to the prospect week after week, with no change in results.

In the end, when the sales rep finally stopped calling, no decision was ever made. What a terrible waste of time and energy for everyone!

Chapter 12
How to Ask the Big Question

It's like a sporting event where no final outcome was ever arrived at — they simply ran out of time or the teams stopped showing up.

It's like watching a three-hour movie and leaving before it's over.

Handling indecision is an extremely important aspect of asking for the order. It should be included in your sales training sessions. And here is where you can start.

Ask each person on your sales team to tell you how they would respond if their prospect said this to them.

"I haven't made a decision yet. Call me next week."

Or perhaps:

"I'm not sure at this point. I'll contact you as soon as I have made a decision."

Once again, write down on a black board or easel what each meeting attendee says and discuss with the group the pluses and minuses of each response. To help them, you might offer the following response as an alternative for them to use.

For any of your representatives who struggle with indecision and find it difficult to quickly and effectively respond to this obstacle, your alternative may be the most important thing you teach them.

I call it "***quantifying the indecision***."

Ask for a volunteer to play the role of a prospect that can't make a yes or no decision and you be the sales representative. Ask your group to observe how you handle the prospect's indecision. It might go something like this:

> Your volunteer (acting as the prospect): "Let me think about it and I'll call you next week."
>
> You: "Mr. Prospect, I certainly appreciate your wanting to take time to carefully consider all of the options before you make your final decision. But as you think about my proposal, may I ask you a question?"
>
> Prospect: "Certainly."
>
> You (here it comes): "If you were to grade my proposal on a scale of one to ten, with ten being the highest, what number would you give it?"
>
> Prospect (after thinking a moment or two): "Well, I guess it would be an eight."
>
> You: "Eight. That's a pretty good number. But tell me, what do you believe we need to do to make that eight into a ten?"

The answer your prospect makes to your last question will provide you with the final piece of information you need to complete the decision-making process.

In many instances, it may lead you to summarize your previous conversations with your prospect, identifying benefits as you go (and using those testimonials), asking for a progression of common agreements.

Chapter 12
How to Ask the Big Question

It may also uncover a hidden objection you were not aware of. Once it has been voiced, it becomes something you can address.

The most important thing, however, is that you have shifted the course of the conversation from one of indecision back to the issues that need to be addressed in order to remove that indecision.

"What do we need to do to change that eight to a ten?"

Notice also that I said "we," versus "I" or "you." Solid business relationships are true business partnerships. It's a *we* business.

So, whether you're suggesting "what we should do now" or asking "what do we need to do now," you'll discover that both can play an important role in asking the big question — and gaining another customer.

There's a **Fine Line** between a **GROOVE** and a **RUT**

13 TWENTY-ONE
FINE LINE INDICATORS

As I mentioned earlier in this book, once you start to see the sales volume begin to drop with some of your star players, they may have already crossed over that fine line and find themselves in a rut.

Ideally, if you can identify when someone on your team is beginning to slip **before** their productivity declines, you'll be in a better position to help them maintain a peak performance level.

You should always be looking for those indicators of where you can step in to help.

So what are some of the indicators that may suggest that an individual may be sliding from a groove toward a rut? What are some of those signals that you need to look for?

Several years ago I had the occasion to meet with a group of sales managers to discuss sales management. We all agreed that managing a sales force was a continual work-in-progress. It was never ending. As sales managers, we were the coaches, mentors, disciplinarians and cheerleaders all rolled into one.

The idea of simply setting a course of direction and letting our sales representatives run with it never seemed to work satisfactorily. Similarly, the idea of letting our sales people set their own course of direction didn't produce the desired results either.

From all the questions that arose from our group discussions, one question drew the majority of our attention. We all were experiencing the same problem — keeping our top performers at their highest level of productivity.

It was not uncommon for each of us to have a top performer one year, who slipped into a mediocre performance the following year. We also had sales people who historically were high producers and had built a solid core of clientele. But as the years went by, some veterans began to lose their competitive edge.

It was at that time that I began to develop a list of ***fine line indicators*** to give me advanced warning that someone who was working for me might be approaching the fine line.

I am not saying that the following list of indicators provide certainty for predicting a productivity decline. However, my list did give me a starting point to focus on. Perhaps it will do the same for you.

1. Reluctance to change. This one heads the list and can affect anyone, especially veteran sales people. Showing a reluctance to change may mean someone is getting burned out or may simply believe that their way

Chapter 13
Twenty-One Fine Line Indicators

is the only way. This is possibly the hardest indicator to address. Demonstrating that new sales techniques really work and can make selling enjoyable again may be the best way to change the individual's thinking. They need to read this book, cover to cover.

2. Declining list of prospects. A declining list of prospects can signal a declining interest in doing the hard work of prospecting for potential new customers and the lack of soliciting referrals. Chapters Five, Ten and Eleven could be of great help.

3. Looking for shortcuts to create sales. Taking shortcuts during a personal sales visit occurs when someone is not using a selling agenda. The result is that the business relationship, if established, becomes more of a buyer-seller arrangement rather than a true business partnership. Continued growth with this customer is limited. They need a selling agenda. Chapter Seven can help get them back on track.

4. Defaults on sales contests. These individuals can be great performers, but avoid public competition. They incorrectly believe defaulting on sales contests provides them with an excuse, if they perform poorly. Although this whole book would be of value to such individuals, Chapter Four would be particularly beneficial. Also, Chapter Twelve.

5. Becoming less interactive during sales meetings. This type of reaction is part of the "not wanting to try new ideas" thinking. Simple exercises, such as those discussed in Chapter Two, can be particularly effective.

6. Inconsistent sales performance. You may see an individual's sales results up one month and down the next. They break quota one month and miss it the next. Their business performance becomes a roller-coaster. This is typical of anyone who successfully closes a prospective sale, but fails to replace that prospect with a new one. The result is that they have to spend every other month rebuilding a prospect list. See Chapters Five and Six.

7. Hesitating to embrace new products. These folks tend to stay in a comfort zone of perceived sales success. Chapter Four will get them involved in new product/service introductions.

8. Selling on personality alone, rather than professional knowledge. Injecting personality into a business relationship can be beneficial, but should not be the sole reason you have this customer. Chances are, if the key contact at the customer leaves, the business may be lost. Incorporating a selling agenda (Chapter Seven) can avoid this.

9. Performing poorly on inherited accounts. See indicator number eight. It's likely that the same causes and the same remedy apply.

10. Hesitating to ask for help when there is an obvious need. Most of us do not like to admit that we need help with something. As the manager, you must take the initiative. There may be something in each chapter to help this individual.

11. Knowing little about his customer's business. Here the customer relationships tend to be shallow. Again it is more of a buyer-seller, rather than a partnering relationship. Such an individual needs to develop and use more informational questions. You might like to reference Chapters Nine and Eleven.

12. Using cold calling as the primary means to develop prospects. This individual works hard but not smart. Start with Chapters Five and Six.

13. Tending to "wing it" during sales calls. Individual does not use any kind of selling agenda or do any pre-sales call preparation. See Chapter Seven.

14. Failing to use any kind of people network to promote his work. The ideas in Chapters Two and Three can change this overnight.

15. Hesitating to take on a leadership role. This individual needs to be encouraged to challenge and stretch his or her abilities. Any one of the roll-playing exercises in this book will provide the opportunity for that person to demonstrate leadership.

16. Poor organization. Developing a selling agenda will have an enormous positive affect for this individual. Chapter Seven will be particularly helpful (as well as Chapter Four).

17. Failing to use or take notes during sales calls. You may find that this person is weak in taking care of details that can result in missed opportunities. Focusing on the use of informational questions in Chapter Nine is a great place to start.

18. Failing to ask current customers for referrals or testimonials. See Chapters Five and Ten.

19. Failing to practice sales presentations. This indicator is similar to someone who wings it during a sales call. Chapters Four and Seven will help.

20. Uncomfortable in role-playing. Performing in front of one's peers can create anxiety for many. You may also see similar anxiety when you, as their manager, accompany them on sales calls. That's why I included the exercises in Chapters Two and Three. They make role-playing easy.

I think you will discover that the indicators I have identified above can be addressed using the training ideas I have talked about in this book. As their coach, mentor, disciplinarian and cheerleader, you are in a position to give your sales team the tools to overcome any deficiencies you suspect they may have.

Before we leave the subject of fine line indicators, I'd like to mention another indicator that should be added to the list.

Fine Line Indicator 21: Failure to submit sales call reports.

I am a very strong proponent of sales reports. And although sales representatives in general do not like to fill out reports, such reports are an important business tool. Four specific benefits come to mind.

First, reporting enables the sales representative to document his or her work. It's impossible for anyone to remember everything that occurs during a sales call, and a systematic yet simple reporting criteria can ensure that all relevant details are documented. It can ensure that important information does not fall through the cracks.

Chapter 13
Twenty-One Fine Line Indicators

Second, reporting provides a history of activity that can be useful when issues need to be revisited. This history is especially important if a new representative assumes responsibility for an existing account.

Third, the information contained in sales reports can provide a resource for market research. Not only can you learn the industrial makeup of your customers, but you can also identify customer demographics, who the decision makers are, what products and services are being promoted the most, what products and services are not being presented, how long it takes to close sales, and a wealth of other information.

And finally, sales reports offer a great opportunity for you to teach and train your sales people. Reports tell you how your sales people sell. They document successes and failures. They help you identify many of the other fine line indicators listed above.

By responding to sales reports you receive, you can reinforce and share with others their recognized strengths. And you can help individuals improve their weaknesses, through constructive and empathetic coaching and instruction.

If you do not have any type of systematic reporting system in place, I urge you to start one. It's the best way to learn what your sales team is doing. You may be amazed at what you read.

Here's an example.

About fifteen years ago, I worked for a company that required written reports from its sales force. Having just assumed the management position for an organization

There's a **Fine Line** between a **GROOVE** and a **RUT**

involving over 100 sales representatives, I was anxious to become familiar with our sales activities and learn more than just who our customers were and what we were selling to them.

To obtain a snapshot of my sales force in action, I asked each of my sales managers to obtain and send me a copy of a daily sales report from each of their sales people. I selected January 14th as the day I wanted to read about. The date I selected was arbitrary. I simply wanted to learn what each of the 100 sales people did on that very same day.

As I began to receive and read the reports sent from my managers, a picture quickly began forming in my mind. From the reports received for that one day, I identified a number of indicators that served as a basis for putting together a sales training program.

Here are some of the things I learned:

The report form we were using had been designed to accommodate eight personal sales calls. It was obviously assumed that anyone making more than eight calls on a given day would create a second page.

To my astonishment, almost 60 percent of my sales force made exactly eight calls on January 14th.

Was this a coincidence? I doubt it.

Because the form provided spaces for eight calls, my company unknowingly was sending the message that after eight calls were made, the day could be ended. Conversely, if you hadn't made eight calls, you had better get in a couple of "quickie" calls, before you finished the day.

Chapter 13
Twenty-One Fine Line Indicators

The point here is you should not overlook how you design your reporting criteria. You may be inadvertently sending the wrong message.

In reading the reports from January 14th, I also discovered that a significant percentage of the sales calls resulted in failure to make contact with the targeted prospect. It appeared that I had a large number of sales people driving around in cars making cold calls.

I learned that very few sales people were asking for and obtaining referrals and testimonials. Or, if they were, they were keeping it a secret.

Less than a third listed the specific objective(s) of the call. In most instances, the reporting of specific results were vague.

Only a small number of representatives were scheduling follow-up sales calls.

In general, with a few exceptions, the lack of a selling agenda was apparent.

What I learned from reading those 100 sales call reports was extremely instrumental in helping me develop a sales training program to address the sales skills that were most important to my sales force.

If you have a sales force, try this same exercise. You may be pleasantly surprised. And in the process, you may identify some fine line indicators to address with sales individuals as well as with your entire sales staff.

There's a Fine Line between a GROOVE and a RUT

14 THE RULES OF THE GAME

I offer the following ***Fine Line Rules of the Game***, presented throughout the book, to help your sales team stay above the fine line.

> **Fine Line RULE # 1**
>
> The best person to teach new ways to improve your employees' performance is **you**.

As a business owner and manager, no one has a better understanding of your business, its operations, its vision, and its desires than you do. There is no one better than you to share these thoughts and ambitions with your sales force and other employees. Although recruiting outside professionals to help you improve performance can bring many benefits, it's equally important for you to utilize your own talents and knowledge to build your team of players (Chapter One).

Fine Line
RULE # 2

Seize every opportunity to promote your business and what you do.

No one will talk about your business unless you start the conversation. Look for those opportunities where you can begin a meaningful dialogue with friends, acquaintances, associates, colleagues and even strangers. You will be amazed at how often these opportunities present themselves and the positive results your conversations will produce. It's called "networking" (Chapter Two).

Chapter 14
The Rules of the Game

Fine Line
RULE # 3

> When explaining what you or your company does, create a mental picture for your listener.

You know your business very well. You know all the jargon of the industry. But chances are your listener does not. It is so easy when explaining your business to use terms that are familiar to you, but may be confusing to others. By using examples commonly recognized by those who you are talking to, you will provide a clear and lasting impression of what your business is all about (Chapter Three).

Fine Line
RULE # 4

> The best way to tell your story is with features, advantages, and benefits.

Whether you are talking about your total business, a part of your business or a product or service you provide, by explaining in terms of what is the feature, how does it work to the user's advantage, what is the resulting benefit and connecting the benefit to an identified need, you will have expressed yourself in the most impactful way (Chapter Four).

> **Fine Line**
> **RULE # 5**
>
> A current customer will be very receptive to giving you a referral. All you need to do is ask.

People enjoy helping others. Good customers enjoy helping their suppliers who provide them sources of quality goods and services. Your customers are ideal candidates to lead you to potential new customers, and they will respond favorably when asked. And if, in turn, you can refer potential customers or other resources to them, you will create a deeper, more meaningful relationship with each of them (Chapter Five).

Chapter 14
The Rules of the Game

Fine Line
RULE # 6

In your very first statement, give the person you are calling a reason to **want** to talk with you.

First impressions are lasting impressions, whether you are making a telephone call or a personal visit. Never assume your listener is prepared to listen to what you have to say. They need a reason (Chapter Six).

Fine Line
RULE # 7

If you want your sales organization to perform at the top of its game and present the best possible image of your company, teach them **your** selling agenda.

By not equipping your sales force with your selling agenda, you run the risk of each of them using their own agenda; one that may not be consistent with your goals and objectives. Or worse, they may have no agenda at all. Their probability of success will be greatly diminished (Chapter Seven).

> **Fine Line**
> **RULE # 8**
>
> A successful customer relationship begins by establishing your credibility with your business prospect.

Business relationships begin with mutual trust and respect. Credibility is the foundation from which all things are built. It should be the first objective in your selling agenda (Chapter Eight).

> **Fine Line**
> **RULE # 9**
>
> Customer testimonials are powerful selling tools that are easy to obtain. Just **ask** for them.

Think about all those occasions when you have purchased something that you originally heard about from a friend who had a positive experience with it. Now think about your business being talked about in the same way. Demonstrating your value through third-party endorsements makes a big impression on those who are evaluating your services (Chapter Ten).

There's a Fine Line between a GROOVE and a RUT

> **Fine Line**
> **RULE # 10**
>
> Ask for the order.

If you don't, who will (Chapter Twelve)?

15 THREE THINGS

Over the years, there have been literally hundreds of books written about how to market products and services and how to promote a business. Many discuss how to develop in-depth strategic plans and utilize marketing budgets wisely.

And although I am a strong advocate of having a sound and well designed marketing plan in place, I realize that many organizations have only limited funds to dedicate to marketing initiatives.

What I have tried to demonstrate in this book is that there are a number of things a business can do to enhance the opportunities to generate revenue that do not require large marketing budgets.

In fact, the ideas that I have presented in this book require no budget at all.

Thinking about the fourteen chapters you have just read, perhaps one aspect stands out more than anything else does. The ideas I have expressed are simple, straightforward, easy to teach, and easy to execute. This is certainly not rocket science.

Yet, why is it that so few businesses and the people in those businesses who are in selling situations actually use them on a consistent basis?

I'm not sure.

But I ask you to try these ideas. And I ask you to teach your sales force how to use them as well.

I guarantee that you will see an improvement in their performances. I guarantee that if any one of them is approaching that fine line, if they appear to be slipping into a rut, by teaching them how to employ these simple communication techniques, you will have taken a major step in putting them back on track to finding their groove again.

Besides, what is the alternative?

I would also suggest that you include non-selling employees in this training. They are all ambassadors for your business. Teaching them how to explain their business to others will bring dividends.

One thing is certain. If someone in their professional life has not already experienced either approaching or crossing that fine line that separates a groove from a rut, they will at some time in the future.

And the reason is that nothing ever stays the same. Change is continuous and often outside of our control.

Chapter 15
Three Things

Change can be caused by economic pressures, increased competition, new technology, a better-educated consumer or a combination of these and other factors. And as business professionals, you and your sales force must be prepared to meet these changes on a daily basis.

When success becomes increasingly more difficult, smart professionals return to the basics to sharpen their skills. That is what I have tried to present in this book.

As a final exercise, take a look at the following checklist and see how you and those who promote your business fare.

Fine Line Checklist —

___ Do you take advantage of your communication network, the valuable circles of friends and business acquaintances you have, by engaging them in conversations about your business?

___ When you explain your business to someone, are you sure that they gain a solid understanding of what you do?

___ Do you present your products and services to prospective clients in terms that they can relate to?

___ Are you wasting time making unprepared cold calls?

___ Do you utilize the knowledge and credibility of your customers and circles of influence to help you create new clients?

There's a Fine Line between a GROOVE and a RUT

___ Do you obtain and use referrals and testimonials at every opportunity?

___ Do you accomplish something positive on every sales call and personal customer visit you make?

___ If someone asked you what makes your business credible, could you tell them?

___ Do you know what you should know about each of the customers you serve?

___ Are you doing everything you can to improve your performance and the performance of those who promote your business every day?

How you greet people, how you explain your business, how you present a product or a service, how you facilitate a sales call, how you ask and use referrals and testimonials; this is all pretty basic stuff.

I'd like you to consider the following. I hope you will grant me this one commercial.

You have just purchased this book for yourself and you have just read it. If you believe there is value in it, and I hope you do, I'd like you to buy and give a copy to each person who is in a marketing or sales position in your company.

If just one idea in this book generates one new long-lasting customer for one of your sales people, your purchase will have been worthwhile. Having them read the book will also make any training sessions you conduct that much more impactful.

Chapter 15
Three Things

Each time I have presented these ideas in training sessions and interactive workshops to business owners and sales professions, I have received an enthusiastic and receptive response. I believe you will have the same results.

I also encourage your comments. Any thoughts, ideas, suggestions or questions you have for me can be sent to my e-mail address at finelinebook@gmail.com. Or, come visit and post your comments on my weblog, **above the Line**, at http://kittredge.blogs.com. They will all be answered and appreciated.

I'd like to conclude with this final thought.

I was once asked by a business colleague what I thought was the most important advice I could give to a business owner, a marketing professional, or a sales representative regarding promoting their business. In other words, if I had to boil down into a few sentences all that I have read about marketing, all that I have heard from other marketing professionals plus what I have learned through my own personal experiences, what would I say?

It's a great question.

Without hesitation, I answered my colleague's question with a question of my own.

What are the three most important things your next customer needs to know about you?

My advice was the following answer, the **Last Fine Line RULE.**

The Last Fine Line RULE

Tell them who you are.

Tell them what you do.

Then tell them what you can do **for them**!

The key is how well you do each of those ***three things***; how well you can articulate and execute this basic marketing message. I think you will discover that whenever you have established a new customer or created a stronger relationship with a current customer, you will have conveyed this message extremely well.

And at the same time, you will have demonstrated your ability to stay above the fine line that separates a groove from a rut.

ABOUT THE AUTHOR

Mr. Kittredge, a graduate of the University of Virginia, has over 25 years experience in sales, marketing, business development, and management. He has held positions as a sales representative, branch sales manager, Regional Vice-President, Vice-President of Corporate Development, Vice-President and Senior Vice-President/Director of Marketing, and Business Unit President. During a period from 1986 to 2001, he championed three new business ventures for the companies he was employed with.

In 1999, Mr. Kittredge's marketing efforts resulted in national recognition by the prestigious ***Kiplinger Letter*** for the products that he was promoting.

He has managed sales forces as large as 110 professionals, a twelve-person marketing team, as well as personally executed the total marketing and sales efforts for smaller companies. His areas of expertise include client development, sales, marketing strategy and implementation and business strategy.

The information presented in ***There's A Fine Line Between A Groove And A Rut*** is the result of Mr. Kittredge's personal selling, marketing and business management experience with the acknowledgement of the many colleagues and mentors who have helped him along the way.

Most recently, Mr. Kittredge has provided marketing counsel to entrepreneurs planning to start new businesses and small business owners. He also has conducted training sessions and interactive workshops on how to effectively promote one's business, products and services, drawing on a number of ideas presented in this book.

How to Order:

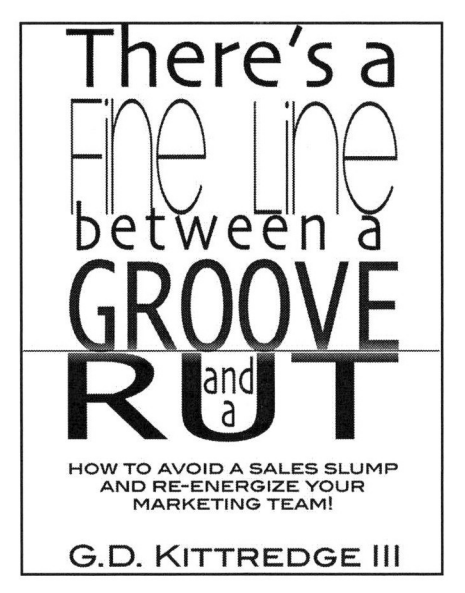

Additional copies of *There's a Fine Line Between a Groove and a Rut* can be ordered online at:

www.WMEBooks.com

Or, by calling toll-free: 1-877-947-BOOK

Ask for it at your local bookstore by title, author name, or ISBN 0-9765304-4-9

For more information on quantity purchases, discounts, and special programs, please contact:

> Special Book Orders
> Windsor Media Enterprises, LLC
> 150 Lucius Gordon Drive
> West Henrietta, NY 14586
>
> info@wmebooks.com

The author invites your comments. Really. Contact him at:

> finelinebook@gmail.com

Or visit his weblog, **above the Line**, at:

> http://kittredge.blogs.com